Interpretation In A Digital Age

Understanding the range of digital technologies available for heritage interpretation

Paul Palmer

Neil Rathbone

Barry

Thanks for your help.
Here's to the future.

neil

Copyright © 2017
Paul Palmer, Neil Rathbone
All rights reserved.
ISBN: 1533253072
ISBN-13: 978-1533253071

Updated: 17th July 2017

To our wives, Lesley and Kate, who offered so much encouragement and support in our business venture and in the writing of this book.

Contents

About the Authors.. iii

Introduction...v

Chapter 1 Handheld Guides.. 1

Key Knowledge - Chapter 1.. 6

Chapter 2 Bring Your Own Device...9

Key Knowledge - Chapter 2.. 14

Chapter 3 Apps and Interactives... 17

Key Knowledge - Chapter 3.. 24

Chapter 4 Working with Media.. 27

Key Knowledge - Chapter 4.. 38

Chapter 5 Webcams... 41

Key Knowledege - Chapter 5...45

Chapter 6 Location and Proximity Triggering......................... 47

Key Knowlege - Chapter 6..62

Chapter 7 Accessibility, Inclusivity, and Mindfulness............. 65

Key Knowledge - Chapter 7.. 80

Chapter 8 Remote, Outdoor and Unattended......................... 83

Key Knowledge Chapter 8..92

Chapter 9 Phone and WiFi Signals... 95

Key Knowledge - Chapter 9... 106

Chapter 10 Standards and Intellectual Property.................. 109

Key Knowledge - Chapter 10... 118

Chapter 11 A New Creative Toolbox......................................121

Key Knowledge - Chapter 11... 132

Chapter 12 Project Management..135

Key Knowledge - Chapter 12... 152

Jargon Buster... 155

About the Authors

Paul Palmer

Paul was born in 1955 and his earliest memories are of watching birds in the garden. This fascination for wildlife has continued to the present day where he is a very active volunteer within the wildlife community. An aptitude for repairing the family television as a boy was the first indication that his professional career would be as an engineer where he worked on technologies ranging from nuclear power to the humble fuse, and many things in between.

He is a self-confessed geek and a passionate communicator on technical and wildlife topics with over 40 publications to his name, which, he says, proves that at least some engineers can write clearly!

Neil Rathbone

Born in 1955, Neil started his career in the 1970s in marketing and business management. Since 1990 he has specialised in the management and communication of technology, both in industry and the public sector. He is neither a geek nor a technophile, but is interested in the way that technology interacts with human cultures and ultimately becomes insidiously pervasive. He has always been keen that people understand the technology that they use, and hence use it wisely.

In his leisure time he is a volunteer flying instructor, and has a keen interest in social history and archaeology, being a member of several local groups, although he describes himself as fundamentally part of the 'brogues and cream teas' sector of the heritage audience.

Introduction

The genesis of this book was our realisation that the heritage interpretation sector, particularly its creative players, want to use mobile digital technology, but have difficulty finding objective and practical guidance. We all realise that the smartphones in our pockets have opened up a whole new range of information and interpretation possibilities: not only for traditional museums, but more especially for outdoor historical and natural heritage, and for archaeological excavations. However, the use of technology within the heritage sector has often lacked robustness, and that has led to nervousness and caution. Technology suffers from a tendency to over-hype its potential, and later to be disappointed by its limitations, a process known as the 'Gartner hype cycle'. Having said that, it is important to always be looking over the horizon and to think about extracting long-term value from today's investment.

This book will improve your confidence in your own knowledge and understanding, and so help you to make better technology management decisions. We have assumed no technical knowledge and have tried to explain the jargon. We have tried to be objective, and to refrain from promoting our own product and views in the text. Ultimately the choice of technology must be yours, and should be based on you knowing what is best for you, and why.

The story of Info-Point

In 2012, while experimenting with a web-based business idea involving QR Codes, we carried out an experimental installation for visitors to an Iron-Age hill fort. It revealed two major problems. One was that cows will eat QR Codes. The other was that, despite being on a hill in the middle of England, the mobile phone signal was not good enough to stream rich media from the Web to visitors' smartphones, or to download an app.

Further research and testing led us to realise that poor connectivity was a widespread and major issue for heritage sites across the world, effectively restricting their options for digital interpretation. Despite the promises of service providers and governments, connectivity looks to be a long-term problem as heritage sites tend to be away from centres of population, which is where the subscribers are that make mobile masts and broadband viable. Our business idea was dead. Except…

We found a solution. A self-contained device that generates a Wi-Fi signal with a private 'local internet' behind it that looks and behaves like the public internet, so is usable by any nearby web-browsing device. The need for global connectivity disappears. The venue's story can be developed and uploaded to the device using standard web technology. We turned the idea into the 'Info-Point' product and launched it tentatively in 2013. It met with an immediate welcome from frustrated heritage interpreters and managers. The only negative comment was "Where the hell were you the other year! I needed this then!".

We have been unable to solve the cow problem.

www.imfo-point.eu

Handheld Guides

Guides 1

The audio-guide actually pre-dates the digital age, having emerged as early as 1957. These devices were based on reel-to-reel tape players and contained analogue electronics, so offered only a linear 'play and pause' experience, with limited ability to select a topic at will. As they were expensive, their use was restricted to a few major museums.

As the cost and availability of consumer audio devices fell, they became the main media to use for guided tours. The handheld device, either loaned or rented, has gone through several incarnations that have tended to follow the availability and economics of playback devices made for the mass market. From the Sony Walkman to the iPod, suppliers have re-purposed small devices at an economic cost.

In the age of solid-state digital electronics, the bigger suppliers could design their own handsets with the tour semi-permanently 'burned' into the chip. In large volumes, the economics of such dedicated handsets was favourable, and they have no tradeable value, so are less likely to be stolen than a general-purpose consumer device. The traditional method of operation for such hand-held guides is to access each item of content by keying the numbers displayed at key points along the tour. Most systems have some form of accompanying rack on which units are stored and re-charged, and which sometimes provide mass re-programming facilities.

The State of the Art Today

Audio guides are still sold today and have the advantage that you simply listen, while your other senses can be used to take in your surroundings. Although it may today appear a bit low-tech and dated, this technology is well understood and still has an appeal. Audio guides can also be less sound-polluting as they are normally held to the ear.

Portable video devices opened up the possibility of showing both still images and video to enrich the experience, but have the possible drawback that the visitor can end up looking at and listening to the device to the detriment of taking in the heritage directly. They can also be sound-polluting in crowded spaces as they are held away from the body, rather than held to the ear.

A new variation has emerged with the availability of low-cost tablets. Such tablets can be highly sophisticated and can offer interactive content on an easy to see touch-screen. They can be programmed with a native app, making them entirely self-contained, or linked via Wi-Fi to a web-based content source, in which case they can also be integrated with Bring Your Own Device (BYOD) to make a hybrid system that helps to overcome some of the limitations, such as capacity. As well as being hand-held, they can be offered as touch-screen 'kiosk' devices, secured to a wall or plinth for general public access.

While traditional audio-guides are still being sold, and many legacy systems are still in use after years of service, the ubiquity of the smartphone and tablet that will provide the same functionality means that it makes less sense to buy and maintain capital equipment that duplicates the capabilities of the user's own device. As well as the tendency for units to get lost or damaged, the technology of digital electronics is now changing so rapidly that the risk of early obsolescence is high. Indeed, the consumer devices on which some audio guide systems are based, such as MP3 players, are now are being withdrawn as their capability is being incorporated into smartphones and tablets. For example, the once ubiquitous iPod Classic ceased production in 2014.

Practical considerations

Hand-held devices are only suitable for staffed venues where there is a defined entrance and exit so that the devices can be handed out and collected in, and their use to some extent supervised.

Due to the large number of units required, hand-held guides are a significant capital investment. Some vendors offer a 'no capital' option of permanently renting the units so that they become an annual revenue cost, and some even offer income cost-sharing as a way of financing them.

Most of the hardware devices offered are proprietary, and more importantly, their content is often controlled by the vendor, who are consequently able to lock customers into their content production services for updates. Some providers have switched to low-cost standard consumer devices. These present a higher risk of theft so often incorporate alarms that will trigger if the device is taken through the exit. These alarms normally use radio frequency triggers and are a good application for 'beacon' technology and RFID.

Charging time can be an issue, especially during peak periods when you may want to use a unit three or more times in a day. A further issue is that battery life may be reduced as the device ages. The life of rechargeable batteries is normally around 500 to 800 charge/discharge cycles so it is possible to estimate the battery life from this or the manufacturer's stated cycles.

Rapid charging technologies using capacitors instead of batteries are now feasible. These could offer 10,000+ charge cycles, but are likely to have a higher cost.

Any unit handed to the public is susceptible to damage and this can be a major problem. The audio connector for headphones is a common point of failure and some systems add reinforcement to protect the connector. In 2016 Apple announced their retirement of the physical audio connector in favour of a wireless Bluetooth connector, which highlights the manufacturer's experience of weaknesses introduced by connectors. The advantage of wireless headphones in terms of reliability could perhaps lead to a rejuvenation of audio guides in a different form.

Key Knowledge — Handheld Guides

Hand-held devices are reliable and consistent as you control the whole system.

Hand-held devices are are self-contained, so will work anywhere.

Visitors are familiar with the concept of audio guides.

A tour may be difficult to change if your content is navigated by numbers on physical display panels.

You may be locked into the services of the system vendor to make any content updates.

There is always a device loss rate due to accidental damage, willful damage, theft, and absent-mindedness.

Proprietary solutions that are not transferrable to other hardware lock you into one supplier.

Battery life will become gradually reduced over time.

You will need enough units to meet peak demand, including re-charging turn-around times.

Bring Your Own Device

BYOD 2

The smartphone and tablet will soon become the universally normal way to get information. Smartphone and tablet ownership amongst Western adults has now surpassed 75% and among young adults it is virtually 100%. Mobile browsing now exceeds desktop browsing.

The principle of Bring Your Own Device (BYOD) is to use that sophisticated multi-media equipment that is already owned, updated, maintained and carried by the typical visitor. An obvious advantage of BYOD to the venue operator is a reduction in the cost and risk of investing in digital hardware. In many cases users may actually prefer their own device; obvious reasons for this are that they know how to operate it, accessibility reasons - the device may for example have a screen reader or other aid that the disabled user needs. Less obvious are cultural hygiene preferences, where the user may have concerns about cleanliness, especially with devices that touch the skin or hair, such as headphones.

Working Principles

To get content onto a visitor's device you have two main options. One is to provide an app that the user downloads and installs. The other is to provide a web site. In either event, connectivity is required and this again has two options. One is to provide on-site Wi-Fi and the other is to rely on the user's own phone service provider. The first of these is preferable in a number of ways. It will be more reliable and cost-free for the user. For the ambient phone signal to be a workable method all the networks must have a good signal across all of the site. Network providers can occasionally move or amalgamate masts, so there can be no guarantee that a signal currently available will continue to be so. There are also potential cost issues if the user has a data usage limit, or is 'roaming' away from their provider's home network. We have anecdotal evidence that international visitors at major attractions either cannot or will not use their service provider because of concerns about charges. Such 'roaming data' limits and charges are currently an area of both consumer and governmental concern. However, the rest of the world user fear and uncertainty is still a lingering factor. Overall, reliance on external phone service providers, over which you have no control, still carries with it a high degree of long-term uncertainty.

Practical considerations

You can't control the user or their device

Despite its clear advantages, BYOD comes with some challenges. The major one is that you have no control over the system, settings or age of the user device. This means that you cannot use content that requires any form of specialist software or new feature that is not universally available, and that your content must be playable on older devices as well as the latest ones.

An example of such a control issue is that devices now have 'thin client' software that senses if a Wi-Fi is not giving internet access. Such software opens a browser-like screen on the assumption that there is some form of logon required to access the Internet. This automated intervention may not be necessary, and can confuse the user. As internet portals and local Wi-Fi have evolved, devices have changed their thin client behaviours, making the user connection experience something of a moving target. From experience, the best approach is to instruct the user how to get connected by ignoring such thin client behaviour.

Screen resolution and file size

The screens on mobile devices are small and can come in a variety of sizes, so the programming behind mobile web pages needs to be 'adaptive' so that it adjusts such factors as font and image sizes dynamically to suit the user device. When making downloadables such as PDFs you need to make files 'for screen' (around 72 ppi) and not 'for print' (around 300 ppi). You also need to be economical with file sizes. We talk more about video and audio transmission in the rich media chapter, but these and any other downloadables need to keep within what is a reasonable file size for the user to store on their phone.

Noise and the heritage environment

A further consideration is noise. Few users will have a headset with their phone. In some venues, such as places of worship, the background noise of interpretation videos will be detrimental to the ambiance on the site. It can be possible to design the interpretation to minimise disturbance by communicating entirely visually.

What about those without smartphones?

Basic tablets are now so low-cost that a small stock can be loaned or rented to visitors just like hand-held guides, but driven by the BYOD system. Many users change their phones frequently because they get new models as part of their contract. As it is not necessary to have a SIM card in a device in order to use Wi-Fi, unwanted smartphones could be solicited as donations.

Phone battery exhaustion

While powering the visitor's device is arguably the owner's problem, if a visitor is experiencing battery fade then they cannot use their device and so the BYOD interpretation designer has a problem. There are two main solutions for this. One is to provide charging points and leads. Many phones now standardise on the small USB sockets. Mains power sockets are now obtainable that have USB outlets built in. This would be a wise and low-cost feature to include on any new build. The other solution is for the venue to offer supplementary batteries for loan or rent. These devices have a USB output connector, and come with a lead to a micro-USB plug, and usually with a set of adaptors for other connection types. The user simply connects the battery to the phone's charging socket. The batteries are small enough to be carried around in a pocket while they are both powering and charging the phone.

Recharging is a service that visitors might anyway appreciate, and might be an income generating opportunity. We think that in the longer term, the issue of battery fade, which is largely due to the increase in daily phone use, will be resolved by the manufacturers and by changes in user and app behaviours as the problem impacts the user throughout their lives.

Key Knowledge — Bring Your Own Device

BYOD (Bring Your Own Device) requires little or no investment in hardware.

The cost and work of updating and maintenance of hardware is done by the visitor.

You cannot control the user device meaning that you must make your content universal.

You will need to provide on-site connectivity as you cannot assume that users will download apps or content prior to visiting.

Keeping to official W3C web standards, that are supported by multiple platforms, will help to future-proof your system.

The ubiquity of smartphones means that BYOD will probably replace hand-held guides and other venue-owned delivery systems.

15

Apps and Interactives

Apps 3

The term 'app' is a shortening of 'application software' - a computer program that you use as a tool in order to do something specific. Most of us use apps without giving them a second thought: we word-process a document, look up the weather where we are, buy something online, check our social media, make a bank payment. The key point is that an app interacts with you and to do that it needs to connect with you and do some processing on your behalf.

Apps give interpreters the ability to build all kinds of effects, games, challenges and navigable experiences where the user plays a role, so the experience is their personal journey, rather than one that has been fixed by others. We look at the possibilities in a later chapter on creativity.

There are two fundamental types of app: those that are resident in the device, known as 'native apps', and those that are accessed on-demand across the web, known as 'web apps'. 'Hybrid Apps' and 'Progressive Web Apps' are an app that resides on the web, but it has the capability to store some data on the mobile device and work offline.

Native apps

Native apps are ones that are installed within your device, using its computing power to do their work, although they might use the web for things such as updated information. Typically you might use an app to play a game, to get weather information or to do your banking. A browser is a type of native app: one that is dedicated to accessing web sites.

Native apps can in principle access any of the facilities of the device upon which they are running, including hardware facilities such as the GPS, accelerometer and camera. Software and storage, such as saved photographs and contact addresses, might also be accessible to apps. You should be aware that such access is always at the discretion of the user who may block it, so if you commission an app, you should not presume access.

Native apps, because they sit within the user's device, have to be built for a specific operating system such as: Apple iOS, Android, or Windows. This can mean that there is an ongoing maintenance and update requirement throughout the useful life of the app, driven by updates to the operating system that it resides on.

Some devices, notably Apple devices, are locked to their manufacturer's official app store, so that you can only download apps to their device from the one place. All such apps have to be approved by the manufacturer before they are formally published. With the growing awareness of cyber security users can be cautious about software from non-official sources.

Apps are more popular when they are user-centric rather than provider-centric. A national heritage organisation may easily persuade its members to install and use their app as they can use it over time to plan their visits to many properties. An app that only supports a one-off casual visit to a small museum is unlikely to appeal to users.

There is undoubtedly an excessive amount of 'hype' around apps, driven by the media and vendors. It is easy to think that having an app is a mark of professionalism, like having a web site or a telephone - everyone seems to have one. In practice, an app is more of a personal tool that the user will only adopt and use if it brings them clear benefits. Many of the heritage apps that we have seen just present information without bringing the user any additional experiences or interactivity that would justify installing an app. The real challenge with the native app is to engage the visitor more deeply than would otherwise have been possible without the app. Without that it just becomes a substitute for a static web site.

Web apps

Web apps work through a web browser and an Internet connection. If you do your banking or buy something online using your normal browser, you are using a web app because the remote server is doing most of the computing and data storage work. The chief advantage of Web apps is that they are independent of the handheld device type and its operating system, so the web app can work on any mobile device. Web pages that are pure HTML are often referred to as 'static' content as the content is always the same, with no user interaction. The opposite, 'dynamic' content, may change according to user interaction or data loaded from a database. Again, web access to banking accounts is a good example. However, user interaction is unlikely to alter the bank balance displayed!

As web apps operate via the browser, they can be restricted in their access to the device's hardware facilities. For example a modern browser in a modern smartphone can ask the device for its location via GPS in order to trigger localised content. You should also be aware that there is an increasing trend for respecting security and privacy, so many users may not allow such interactions. The device manufacturers may also impose additional restrictions, such as only instructions downloaded through a secure (https) connection may access the GPS. This should not be a technical problem for most web apps, but there may be a financial implication in moving to a https connection.

The question of how users access the Internet also needs addressing. If there is good mobile connectivity, users may be able to access the internet through their own service provider. This may have cost implications, especially for international users, and so creates a barrier for take up. Providing a local WiFi access point has legal and security responsibilities which must be addressed. All public Wi-Fi in the UK must comply with the European Data Retention Directive 2006/24/EC. Ensuring security against malicious users is not a trivial task, so be assured that your IT support services really are on your side when they seem to be suggesting solutions that are more complex or expensive than you expect.

Hybrid apps

Hybrid apps are a cross between native apps and mobile web apps. Essentially it uses browser technologies and programming language, but can run as either a web app or as a native app in a software 'container'.

This means that a single set of code can run on an Internet connected website, and can also run as a native app on any of the major smart device platforms including iOS, Android and Windows. Potentially this is a very attractive solution since it minimises the cost of maintaining separate versions. Each version will still have to be uploaded to each specific platform app store, which will have cost and time implications. Also remember that in reality things are never quite perfect, and minor issues may crop up on particular make and models, leaving the majority of users unaffected. A balance may have to be drawn between frequency of updates to each platform and user satisfaction in order to manage costs.

Progressive Web Apps

These are a new and emerging form of web app that resides on the Web, but has the capability to store some data on the mobile device and to work offline. The user accesses the remote web app via an internet connection, and has the option to save a shortcut icon to their device's home screen, just like any other app. Unlike a simple shortcut to a webpage, the Progressive Web App, will still work if there is no internet connection. In addition itwill download updated data when an internet connection becomes available. This will use some space on a user device and some users might apply their own limits to such storage.

Such apps are downloaded through a web browser and not through an App store. However, note that a secure connection will almost certainly be required along with some user education on how this technology works.Although Progressive Web Apps are a newcomer to the app scene, we think that it has real potential for the heritage community. However, its use is still predicated upon the availability of an internet connection for initial download, although users will be able to continue to use it once they move away from an internet connection.

Do you *really* need an app?

The meteoric rise of smartphone apps has persuaded many venues to commission apps without enough critical thought. Apps are seen as the latest 'must have' item, and so venues are understandably keen to have one. The decision-makers who request an app from their (often reluctant) interpreters are usually enthusiastic users of apps on their own device. However, in many cases the interactive content that would justify an app does not exist, and it would be far better to use another approach. Indeed, some 'apps' that have been commissioned are nothing more than off-line containers for static information that could have been more easily downloaded in another form.

The downside is that apps, particularly native apps, present a number of technical challenges, such as on-site connectivity, and can come at considerable cost to build and to maintain over time. The real killer though is user motivation. Unless an app offers something special it can be insufficiently attractive to the user to take the trouble and risk to access and install it, then have to remove it later. The take-up record of apps built for single-visit heritage experiences is extremely poor, although you would not know it from the claims made by owners and developers. Take-up can be checked by looking at such apps on the app stores, where the number of actual downloads is shown.

Apps that are centred on the user and their ongoing needs, rather than centred on a single venue visit, are much more attractive to users. Examples are national multi-venue heritage organisations that provide an app that enables you to see what venues are nearby, when they are open, and what events that currently have on. Some native apps, by auto-updating when connected to Wi-Fi can thus be used anywhere, anytime, and always have current information. Membership-based organisations can use an app to give benefits and maintain a relationship with their members. The key to success is that the app is user-centred and fills an ongoing need, rather than being limited to serving a single visit.

Key Knowledge — Apps and Interactives

There are two fundamental types of app: native and web. Plus some hybrids.

Native apps can be independent of connectivity by both app and content being stored on the phone.

A native app version will be needed for each popular operating system. Currently at least iPhone, Android, and Windows.

Native apps need an internet connection to enable downloading from an app store.

Web apps need an internet connection all the time, either via Wi-Fi or the mobile phone network.

The download statistics for Apps aimed at single-venues have been poor.

Working with Media 4

The term 'media' refers to non-text forms of communication, such as images. 'Rich' media is used for non-static media such as audio, video, and the more recently emerging capabilities such as interactive games and Augmented Reality, although these are more frequently now called 'interactives'. Rich media presents fairly complex challenges in production and is an area where professional help is going to be either essential, or at least worth considering.

Expectations

One important factor to bear in mind is user expectation. The professionally-designed media content that we experience in our daily lives continually raises the public's expectations. On the other hand, the emergence of social media and online video may be building a greater tolerance for raw unedited and sometimes technically poor video. If you are a major national heritage organisation, then the expectation of professionalism is likely to be high, whereas a visitor to a small volunteer-led museum may have lower expectations.

Another consideration is that most of us have been formally taught, during years of schooling, and perhaps continuing in our professional work, to use written and spoken words to communicate, so we tend to have a high level of competence in text creation. While we may be sophisticated consumers of rich media, we tend to lack in-depth knowledge of the backroom skills used in its creation. While this knowledge can to some extent be acquired by trial and error, and by emulating professional radio and TV, the result may still seem 'amateur'. It is tempting to think that having the equipment is all that's required, and modern technology can seduce us into thinking it's easy, but it still requires knowledge and skill. An example is the length of each shot and the speed of cutting. If you watch professional films and television each shot is only a few seconds long. If you look at amateur videos on the Internet, they tend to have over-long introductions, and each shot lasts several minutes. The difference in effect is very noticeable, even if the viewer does not understand the underlying reason.

Having said that, if you have, or are willing to acquire, the 'soft' skills then modern devices and software open up the possibility to make good quality rich media at very little cost. An investment of time learning production techniques can be enough. However, you may need some additional equipment such as tripods to give steady shots, and directional microphones to record good quality sound.

Formats

Whether professionally produced or DIY, the main technical hurdle in presenting rich media in mobile digital is understanding the optimum playback formats to use. In situations where you own and control the playback device it is enough to prove that something works by testing it once. With mobile digital and BYOD you cannot control the user's device and so you have to be very aware of what will work and what will not across the range of devices. Some types of media have very common standards, such as JPEG images, Portable Document Format (PDF) documents and MP3 sound files. Once you go beyond these, then you need to be careful about the file types used and the many available settings, which can be quite technical.

False testing

A common mistake is to only test on your own smartphone or tablet. Different makes and models of device and operating system support different formats, and even the configuration of a device can determine whether a rich media file will play or not, or be available for download.

Another 'false test' is to upload to an online service such as YouTube or Vimeo. These online 'true streaming' services process the uploaded file in a very sophisticated way. The service can even sense the preferred format of the user device and adapt 'on the fly' to varying connection speeds. These highly sophisticated services have to be constantly updated as technology moves on. For this reason many web sites use such streaming services to host their videos in preference to self-hosting. However, this means that video streaming services are not a valid test environment if they will not be your final hosting system.

Despite the challenges of production, rich media greatly enhances the visitor experience. It not only makes interpretation more entertaining and enjoyable, but also more accessible and educational. A significant proportion of the population are not adept at taking in information from the written word, and we all remember more of what we see and hear.

Audio

It is possible to record audio tours, oral histories and slide presentations with voice-over, using nothing more than a laptop and some software. You are unlikely to achieve the quality of a trained professional and their equipment, but if the budget will not cover external professionals, then modern digital technology is capable of producing a very reasonable result if you approach it with some care. Local educational institutions may offer courses, and may even have specialist units that support heritage and oral history recording.

The best piece of generic advice is to test, test, test. Do not just turn up with the equipment and software and try to do the final recording 'on the fly'. Script if necessary (or have memory jogging notes) and rehearse. Then make short test recordings, output them to final format and play them back to check that the whole system works. Make adjustments to the recording 'studio', microphone position and the file quality until you are happy with the result.

It may be worth investing in, or hiring, a specialist microphone or just a cheap headset. Laptops, smartphones and tablets all have 'omnidirectional' microphones that try to pick up sound from all around. This can include hollow-sounding echo from the room, traffic from outside, and any other noise that your hearing normally discounts, but that will sound weird on a recording where the source cannot be seen. A directional mic or headset will just pick up the voice and exclude background noise.

Fortunately, MP3 has become the standard for sound files on mobile devices, and most such files will play on most devices. It is only worth using higher quality settings if the user device is capable of reproducing that quality, otherwise you are wasting space and bandwidth. We have made some settings recommendations for mobile devices below. If you are departing from these, remember to test on a variety of makes and models including old and new devices.

Video

Video is currently the most technologically fraught aspect of rich media. Despite its long history in broadcast television, video technology is in many ways still 'emerging' as the world moves into digital and high-definition, and at the same time deals with the limitations and constraints of mobile devices. As a result, the technical standards in mobile digital video are to some extent unstable, and are still influenced by recent anti-competitive behaviour of vendors trying to corner the market. This means that interoperability is not as good as it could be. Even the terminology is not always clear: for example 'MPEG4' is used to refer to both a file container and a codec - which are two very different things.

One of the most frequent issues that we encounter is the availability of ever-increasing quality that demands ever-better hardware, ever-bigger storage, and ever-faster connectivity. This clashes with the fact that the population of user devices can be from around two to five years old and so significantly behind the technological curve of a good production house. Also, the amount of data that can be streamed over a busy shared Wi-Fi connection is limited by the laws of physics.

Most of this is invisible to us if all we do is to shoot some video on our phone, and play it back on the same device, as it is bound to be compatible with itself. However, this ease of DIY production and presentation can also lull us into a false sense of video being easier than it is.

There is no simple 'do this' answer to how to prepare a video. You need to understand a little of the factors involved, make a trial version, then test it on a variety of devices. If it works, then it works. If not, then you need to research the technology in more depth.

Production shooting

Always shoot at the highest quality that you or your film production company is capable of. The 'prints' that you make can easily be made to suit the playback medium available. It is not possible to go from a low-resolution or compressed video to higher quality as information is permanently lost in the compression process.

A trained professional and their equipment will nearly always produce a far superior result. If you are limited to amateur shooting, then try to get some basic training, plan your shooting and lighting carefully and do things like use a tripod or at least a steady of some sort. Sound is the area that can most often let productions down, as most consumer devices will not record sound nearly as well as a dedicated microphone.

Editing and output for playback

There is a lot of computer-based software available, including free and Open Source, for video editing and conversion, including adding voice-overs or mixing still or moving images with a recorded oral history. You do not need a sound studio, although a little bit of research and knowledge will go a long way. The software will enable you to take your video original as shot, or as edited, and produce copies or 'prints' in any one of many formats.

Types of playback

There are three fundamental ways to play a video on a device:

- Download and play - The entire file is downloaded, after which you can hit 'play' to see it. This is a safe and low-tech way, but boring for the user due to the wait until downloading is complete.

- Streaming - The video is transmitted to your device in chunks of a few seconds at a time. Each chunk is played then discarded. This is the high-tech way that most online video services work.

- Pseudo-streaming - The video begins downloading then starts to play before downloading is finished. This is the way that most web sites and in-house systems work as true streaming is expensive.

Output formats

Whatever the method of playback, your video needs to be output in a format that the playback device can understand. Additionally there is a need to optimise the format to work efficiently and enable the user device to deliver the video in 'real time' without stuttering. As it is a minefield of confusion, it is best to tackle the settings for video output one step at a time:

File types

These are sometimes referred to as 'file containers' since a video is in fact made up of a number of files, each of which performs a different function. The file container type is identified by the filename extension (the part after the dot). The one to use for mobile devices is .MP4. Other common file type extensions that you may encounter are: .AVI, .ASF, .MOV, .QT, .FLV, .SWF, .3GP.

Codecs

This is the software that does the hard work of converting the camera image into a file and re-converting it back from a file to an image on the screen. It includes a lot of work in compressing and decompressing the information to make it efficient to store and transmit. The codec known as H264 is currently the best one to use for mobile applications. Other codecs that you may commonly encounter include: MPEG4, WMV, VP6, DivX.

Resolution

This is the number of pixels or image dots that there are along the edges of the screen (screen resolution) or the video image (video resolution). They are normally stated long side first. Video is always 'landscape' orientation, so the bigger number is the resolution across bottom of the frame. If the video is played 'full-screen' by holding the device in 'landscape' orientation, then the available resolution is the full screen resolution. If the video is played within a device held in 'portrait' orientation, then the image has to squeeze into the reduced number of pixels available.

These two resolution numbers also determine the ratio or format of the screen. For many years it has been common to use 4:3, but increasingly the widescreen of 16:9 is becoming popular. The exact size to use will always be a compromise as visitors will have different devices, but we currently think of 640x480 as a 'lowest common denominator'.

Progressive 'P' v Interlaced 'I'

Some software may give you the options of 'P' for Progressive, or 'I' for Interlaced, after the resolution - for example 480p. Interlaced is a hangover from the days of cathode ray tube televisions in which alternate lines were traced by the flying dot which then flew back to the top and filled in the other lines. Digital media always uses 'progressive'. If you see jagged edges on moving objects then you have a video that is interlaced. They can be de-interlaced by editing software.

Frame rates

This is the number of still images per second (Frames Per Second - FPS) that make up the video. Higher frame rates will produce smoother video, but at the expense of file size, processing and bandwidth. Moreover, frame rates higher than the user device can play will cause wasted capacity and possibly some additional processing overhead to 'interpolate' to a lower rate, but not produce any increase in quality.

Cinema films have always used 24 FPS, but many modern smartphones are capable of 30 FPS, so it is normal to choose one of these. Another consideration is the frame rate at which the video was shot as matching that perfectly will be better than, for example, trying to get 30 frames out of 24. The frame rate can be much lower (eg. 10 FPS) if you are prepared to accept some jerkiness, or have static slides rather than full motion video.

If you are using animation or stop-motion, then the original frame rate or an exact multiple of the shooting rate is best (eg. 5 FPS to 25 FPS, or 10 FPS to 30 FPS).

Bit rates

Bit rate is the number of bits per second that you need to transmit from server to device in order to play the video continuously in real time. It is an important setting as it affects both the final file size, and the bandwidth requirement - in other words it defines the minimum size of the 'pipe' that you will need to provide as your network connection so that the video plays continuously if you are streaming or pseudo-streaming.

The total bit rate is the sum of the image and the sound bit rates. The image bit rate is by far the bigger and more important of the two. Let's look at that first.

The image bit rate normally can be set in your editing/conversion software, but there is a minimum if you are to transmit at the quality that you want. This minimum is determined by the resolution, the frame rate, and the amount of movement or 'live action' in the video, which can be estimated on a scale from 1 (stills or talking head) to 4 (fast motion). There is a basic rule of thumb formula for the minimum; from this you can see the factors that affect the video bit rate:

Resolution Horizontal x Resolution Vertical x frame rate x compression constant x movement factor (1 to 4) = bit rate

The file size is less important, but if you exceed the user device's file capacity then you will hit problems. The formula for this is: Bitrate x duration = filesize

Most editing software will produce only constant bit rates, but more advanced and professional editing suites can encode variable bit rates, which can improve efficiency by adjusting the bit rate during playback according to the amount of movement between frames. This optimises quality and speed.

Key Knowledge — Working with Media

'Rich' media is a loose generic term for content that is not static - audio, video, animations, interactives etc.

Most of us do not have the level of production skill and technical knowledge to produce high quality rich media.

It is possible to produce usable content with consumer digital devices.

File formats are an area that you have to understand if your content is to be playable on all the intended devices.

Audio and video files should be between 2 - 5 minutes and kept below 50 Mb

Recommended format for mobile images is:

- File Type: jpeg or png

Resolution:

- File size: max 300 Kb

Recommended format for mobile audio is:

- File type: MP3
- Sampling: 44.1 Khz
- Tracks: 1 or Mono
- Bit depth: 16 bit
- Bit rate: 128 Kbps

Recommended format for mobile video is:

VIDEO SETTINGS

- File type (container): MP4
- Codec: H.264
- Frame Rate: 24 fps or 30 fps
- Resolution: 480p for widest compatibility with older devices up to 1080 for HD
- Interlacing: Always choose 'p' for 'progressive' never 'i' for 'interlaced'
- Screen size: 640x480 (use 1280 x 960 for tablet—aimed versions) or 1080 x 1920 HD
- Video bit rate: 900 kbps up to 1500 kbps where higher resolution

AUDIO SETTINGS

- Codec: AAC
- Channels: 1 (if possible, or 2 if not)
- Sampling rate: 44.1 Khz
- Audio bit rate: 128 kbps

Webcams

One of the more unusual applications of mobile digital is the ability to connect the user to a live webcam. It can give them a view on their own device of something that they may not otherwise be able to see because of security, safety, visibility, time or accessibility. Modern webcams are cheap and capable of high quality images that can be live, recorded or presented as stills. Many modern webcams are made to be viewed over standard local area networks, to which they can be connected wirelessly. They can be controlled by apps to remotely adjust their direction of view and zoom levels. The possibilities of automatic or user-driven digital post-processing offers really exciting creative potential. The fact that the user controls their own personal experience is clearly more appealing than shared screens repeatedly playing pre-programmed content. The fact that it is private on a personal device can also be important. Some users are reluctant to navigate on public displays, knowing that others are observing them over their shoulder.

An accessibility substitute

Many venues struggle with conflicting demands of wheelchair accessibility and ancient - often 'listed' - buildings that do not naturally lend themselves to improving access can't be altered due to their legal status. Although highly desirable, physical access for those with ambulatory difficulties can be impractical, if not impossible.

The provision of a virtual tour is one way of substituting for physical access, but it still leaves the disabled person in a position of being excluded as they are 'left behind' by their able-bodied companions, or of feeling an encumbrance if their companions restrict their own activity.

By providing live view cameras for inaccessible parts of the visitor route, those excluded can still follow their party and so, to some extent, 'share' in the tour as it unfolds. It would even be possible for them to establish a phone connection to one of their party and so continue to be in contact as they watch.

Speciality recordings

Webcams and digital processing can also be used to time shift in various ways. These processes can be automated so that they are done periodically and so produce, for example, a new video every day of action that took place yesterday or last night. Compressing time through time-lapse video is an obvious application. It is also possible to only store images where something was moving and so produce 'edited highlights' of action while skipping periods of inactivity.

In this way, a constantly updated video can be made available that is guaranteed to be interesting and has a known time to run, that is realistic in terms of visitor dwell time.

Naturecams

Nests and other sensitive places that cannot support visitors can be streamed to them. For places that are required to be kept secret, the use of Wi-Fi and networking means that the visitors can be not only a long way away, but also be kept unaware of where the activity is taking place. Specialist night-lighting and use of the infrared or ultraviolet spectrum for imaging can enable sights that are simply not available to the human eye.

Microscopes are another type of interpretation aid that can be broadcast to multiple visitors. This overcomes the issue of crowding and taking turns to see something. Digital microscopes are in reality just specialist webcams and can be fed into a BYOD system.

Interactive take-aways

The visitor need not be restricted to passive viewing. They can be involved in interactive image-making. Having users pan and zoom webcams is not a practical proposition due to multiple conflicting inputs. However, a facility to enable screen shots to be easily captured gives each visitor the ability to 'take' pictures that they can then own and share on social media. It is possible for the user to digitally post-process images 'Instagram-fashion' to add effects. An interesting example would be the use of 'green screen' backgrounds to superimpose images of choice. Visitors could, for example, take selfies while being photo-bombed by characters from the past.

Key Knowledge — Webcams

See the unvisitable 'live': nests and burrows, microscope views, dangerous places

See the unseeable: time-lapse, daily highlights, night vision.

A substitute access where wheelchair access is not practicable.

Save images as a take-away.

Modify images interactively - green-screen selfies.

Location and Proximity Triggering

6

Location

Imagine if your smartphone, instead of being a dumb audio-visual playback machine, behaved more like a smart human guide: advising you about the spot where you are standing, telling you the stories behind the things that you are looking at, sensing what you might be interested in without you having to make any navigation inputs other than to wander around. The modern smartphone or tablet can do this because it can be aware of its location and can 'push' appropriate content to the user.

Triggered content can be made so that it is only discoverable on-site and at a specific location, which is a way of giving value to those who have made the effort to visit, or paid the ticket price.

There are now several technologies capable of triggering location-specific content. Each of these technologies opens up possibilities for the design of exciting interpretive experiences. Some are very simple and low-cost to implement, while others are technologically sophisticated. Each has its limitations and pitfalls. Let's look at them one by one.

Position and orientation

What is it?

Using the same technology that vehicle 'satnav' systems use, modern smartphones can determine their position in space by receiving and measuring signals broadcast from constellations of navigation satellites orbiting the earth. This can be augmented by accelerometers in the device that can sense movement and gravity, so can add more precise position, and also sense the device's orientation.

How does it work?

A smartphone can determine its latitude and longitude and also its height relative to earth by measuring signals from constellations of earth-orbiting satellites. Smartphone apps and browser pages can request this position information from the phone's satnav system. The latitude and longitude can then be used to locate the user on a 'georeferenced' map, or to trigger a particular set of information that is specific to the user's location.

Most modern phones can also detect acceleration, so can keep track of your position for a few minutes since the last satnav 'fix'. The accelerometers can also detect orientation with respect to gravity. This orientation information opens up possibilities for direction-sensitive content such as Augmented Reality (AR), where you use your phone as a kind of movable window to 'look around' content which is superimposed onto reality.

Confusingly, satellite position technology is known by several names: Satnav, GNSS (Global Navigation Satellite System - the generic term used by techies but not the public), GPS (Global Positioning System - essentially the original American constellation and so, like 'Hoover', the original proprietary name). Other global constellations in use are GLONASS (Russia), Galileo (EU), Beidou (China).

Problems and pitfalls

Navigation satellite signals are inherently very weak and are easily blocked or suffer interference. A good view of most of the sky is the normal requirement, so coverage at your site may not be good enough - certainly not indoors. Accuracy is generally to a few metres, which is not good enough for individual objects, but is OK for big outdoor spaces. You need to allow for the fact that the calculated position can jump around.

There are now several global systems and some regional ones, plus some 'augmentation' systems that use geo-stationary satellites to improve accuracy, so knowing where in the world it is to be used and which systems visitors are likely to have available in their handset is a significant factor. In essence, you cannot guarantee availability or accuracy.

Older devices or browsers may not have satnav capability. The user may have satnav turned off, or privacy settings set to 'high', which may prevent their browser getting location information from the phone, so you should always provide a fallback option.

Accelerometers measure acceleration and translate that into movement, rather than measuring absolute position. This means that they need to start from a known position or 'datum'. For location information, this datum can be the latest satellite 'fix', which can be updated. For orientation information, a method is needed to establish a datum. An example is that some Augmented Reality (AR) systems get the user to register a real-world object or image on their phone's camera with a virtual one ghosted onto the screen, in order to synchronise the two worlds at the start of the experience.

Ways to use it?

The best application for positioning is to simply locate the visitor on a map. If the visitor does not have internet connectivity then a public mapping service such as Google Maps will not work, but you can design your own map and georeference it such that a dot can be placed at the user location. The beauty of this is that the map is still useful even if the lack of a satellite signal means that the dot is missing. The phone's accelerometers will often update the position for a while if the satellite signal is intermittent.

It is also possible to integrate a search or select facility so that icons are placed on a map as a result and the user can see their location in relation to the things they want to see.

Augmented Reality (AR) has that 'wow' factor when it uses position and orientation information to give a moveable window onto its virtual world. However, you should have a fall-back such as finger-dragging in case the orientation technology is not present or not functioning in the user device.

Position v Proximity

Satellite positioning is an 'absolute positioning' technology in that it has to determine where you are. The following sections are all 'proximity' technologies that work by establishing that you are near to something, without needing to establish your position. Proximity technologies can thus be applied to objects that don't have a fixed location, such as travelling exhibitions, or collections that are frequently re-arranged, as well as inherently moving objects such as vehicles.

Static URLs

The following sections describe technologies that often work by sending a web address or URL (Universal Resource Locator) to the smartphone. The URL is what tells your phone to open a specific web page or play a specific sound or video file etc. It is obviously important that the content remains available at that URL over time, or the system will cease to work. This means that you should ideally control that web address, and not reference addresses that are under the control of others. There is another 'gotcha' in that many Content Management Systems auto-generate a URL from a page title, and will change it if the title changes. There is normally a facility to override this and create your own 'static' URL that will not change. Some systems can generate intermediate URLs, often known as URL shorteners, that, as well as enabling you to manufacture short, user-friendly web addresses, are re-programmable to always redirect the user's browser to the intended content, even if the location of the content changes.

QR codes

What are they?

'Quick Response' or QR codes are a development of the more familiar barcodes found on retail products. In order to carry more information they have two dimensions so appear as a chequerboard pattern. They have been around since the 1990s and are used a lot in advertising to help users go from printed material to a website. Although their demise has often been anticipated, they remain common, mainly because they follow an open standard, so are universally compatible with any QR Code reader app. There are many free online apps to generate QR code images from URLs, and you can print them on a normal printer, so they can have virtually no cost.

How do they work?

The user needs a standard QR code reader app (available free) on their phone. They initiate the app and point their phone's camera at the QR code, which is then 'read' by the reader app. The deciphered QR code consists of text characters. If that text is a web address (ie. it begins http://) then the app launches a browser and takes the user to the URL, which could be a web page, or another type of web resource, such as a video. An app could be designed to use the deciphered text to trigger specific content from the app or from the web.

What to look out for?

Although QR codes are very common, and should work on almost any smartphones that have a camera function, not everyone will have a reader app on their phone, or know how they work.

The camera has to get a clear image, so don't put them too far away, or behind glass orlaminate where reflections, especially of lights, may obscure the image. They can have some built-in redundancy, which makes them more reliable. People sometimes alter them for aesthetic reasons, which generally decreases their reliability.

Ways to use them?

QR codes can be printed quite small (about 20 mm square is the minimum size) so can be easily attached to artefacts or images. This could be useful if you have a large number of similar items such that it would be difficult for the visitor to know which one they are looking at. Having said that, operating the reader app and pointing the camera to get a good image is fiddly.

NFC tags

What are they?

A Near-Field Communication (NFC) is short distance radio technology that works like contactless payment cards. The user holds their NFC-enabled phone next to the tag and it opens the page or resource that is encoded into the tag.

How do they work?

An NFC tag is a very small thin device normally stuck on an object like a self-adhesive label. It is a 'passive' device, powered by a signal from the phone. As such it needs no batteries, and will work in a wide range of temperatures and harsh environments. On receiving an NFC signal from a smartphone, it wakes up and broadcasts a line of text - normally a web address. The user simply holds their phone near to the tag for it to work. You program the tag via a programming app on your phone. During programming you have the option to electronically lock the tag so that it cannot be changed. This prevents tags being hacked, but also prevents you modifying them. NFC is an open standard, so it is not device or software specific.

What to look out for?

NFC requires the visitor to have a phone with NFC capability in its hardware and to have it switched on - which is a battery drain. At the time of writing, Apple devices currently restrict NFC to its ApplePay system, although this is expected to change.

The user has to put their phone within a few centimetres of the tag for it to work, so the tags need to be reachable. It is possible to hide tags by placing them on the back of interpretation panels, providing they are radio-transparent (not metal).

The tags cost a few pence/cents each.

Ways to use them?

NFC tags can be very discreet, and even hidden on the backs of interpretation panels. It is easy to read lots of them as you simply hold the phone near them. Bear in mind that not all phones (or users) will be NFC capable.

Bluetooth Beacons

What are they?

Bluetooth Beacons are a bit like a lighthouse in the sense that they send out a signal irrespective of whether or not anyone is looking. The signal they send is a radio beacon with some short, simple information encoded in it. They vary in size from about that of a pack of playing cards, down to a large thick coin and so are easily hidden. As they transmit continuously, they require a battery or some form of power supply. All forms of Bluetooth beacon require an App of some sort on the phone in order to decipher the signal.

What are they not?

While we may think that we know what Bluetooth is, there exists more than the one type. Most of us probably use the 'wireless data transmission' type of Bluetooth many times a day because we have a wireless keyboard or mouse, a wireless headset or our phone links to our hands-free system in our car. This data transmission Bluetooth requires device pairing for security and is designed for the high data rates of the applications that we have just mentioned. It has in the past been tried as a way of transmitting heritage information to smartphones, but has failed to gain acceptance, as pairing is not something that is easy to set up casually and the hardware and standards have moved on, rendering early applications viable only for older 'feature' phones and not for smartphones. This wireless data sub-set of the Bluetooth standards (technically known as Bluetooth BR/EDR) is normally referred to as 'Bluetooth Enabled'.

'Beacon' technology is based on the Bluetooth Low-Energy (BLE) standards, which are a relatively new sub-set of the overall Bluetooth standards. They are specifically designed for this kind of 'lighthouse signal' broadcast application, and are optimised for low power consumption - hence Bluetooth 'Low-Energy'. Although these BLE standards are part of the Bluetooth family, they are not interchangeable with other Bluetooth standards. Each is specific to its type of application.

How do they work?

BLE Beacons emit short bursts of low-power radio signals. Each beacon has its unique identifier (ID) encoded in its signals. Some types can also encode other information, including URLs.

I

n the case of an ID-only beacon it will always require a dedicated native app on the user device that has a mapping from ID to action for each beacon that you have deployed. Beacons that can transmit URLs (such as Eddystone Beacons) still require an app to read the signal, but can work with a generic app as the URL tells the app what to do.

Receiving devices can also derive an approximate distance to the beacon so can alert the user to the proximity of a point of interest.

Different models of Beacon are available from various manufacturers. Some enable you to programme the transmission power and the period between transmissions as a trade off between user acquisition time and battery consumption.

What to look out for?

The visitor will need a device capable of receiving Bluetooth Low-Energy (BLE) signals. If you are using iBeacons, which transmit only an ID, then the visitor will need a dedicated native app with mapping from ID to action. If you are using one of the Eddystone Beacons and URLs then the visitor can use a generic app. If you are using an Info-Point as the content source, they will have to be connected to the Info-Point Wi-Fi signal first.

Some BLE installations have reported problems with signal reflections, especially from display cabinets and blocking from building pillars, confusing the app as to which beacons are nearby. This can be a relatively low-cost technology to test on-site, so this is advisable.

Beacon devices have varying battery life, some claim a year or two, but all will need periodic changing. We recommend instigating an annual change programme. The battery chemistry is likely to stop working if the temperature of the beacon falls close to zero.

Ways to use them?

Beacons are a push technology so do not require any user action other than walking about. They are best used in indoor spaces, due to their batteries. Ideally they should be placed with definite gaps between the transmission ranges of adjacent beacons to avoid multiple triggers. A good application could for example be to provide an introductory video that plays as you enter each gallery or floor of a large building.

Beacon terminology and history

BLE Beacons are a new and evolving technology. The term 'Beacon' or 'iBeacon' tends to be applied haphazardly to any BLE device, which is confusing. iBeacons are a type of BLE first introduced by Apple in 2013. iBeacons are a very low energy form of BLE because an iBeacon does a really simple job: transmitting only a unique identifier. In this respect an iBeacon is very much like a lighthouse.

In 2015 Google introduced the Eddystone Beacon, similar in concept, but able to encode text, URLs and other information inside its transmission. While the Apple iBeacon is proprietary technology, Google released the Eddystone Beacon software as Open Source to encourage novel development.

It is possible for any developer to use the BLE standards to design and build a custom BLE Beacon and a matching application. Such a custom device could be designed to be very impressive in its capability, but it will not be interoperable with other beacons/apps and so will lock the buyer into a single supplier.

Push technology and advertising

Some of the triggering technologies, in particular the early Bluetooth, were enthusiastically seized upon by the advertising sector as a way to push content to passers-by, without their prior consent. This met with user resistance and privacy concerns and could in some parts of the world be in breach of electronic marketing communication laws. This non-consensual approach was always doomed, as unrestricted and effortless access to the user's attention quickly becomes overused, triggering either the user or the device provider to disable the feature entirely. A fundamental principle in push technology, even in heritage interpretation which is for the visitor's benefit, is to seek the visitor's prior consent and to give them the feeling of being in control of their experience, including inviting you to 'push'. Consent is the key.

Over the horizon - profile-triggered interpretation

An exciting prospect is to turn mobile digital on its head, and use it to influence the visitor's real-world experience. Our smartphones already know a lot about us, both from what we set up explicitly, such as our preferences and profiles, and by gathering information through our daily usage. While this can cause negative reactions and raises issues of privacy and protection, the clear trend is that we are gradually becoming more relaxed about machines knowing about us and using that information to serve us in a more personalised way.

We believe that the future will see our devices increasingly share that information with other devices in our surroundings in order that we get experiences that are more personalised to our needs and desires. If our vehicles, domestic appliances and buildings communicate with and respond to us, then future generations will come to expect heritage visits to have this capability. Various technologies such as 'ambient computing' 'wearable computing', the 'Physical Web' and the 'Internet of Things' are all pointing towards integration and interoperability between devices and the free flow of information that was once locked into specific hardware. It is likely that the presence of computer hardware will become ubiquitous, even disposable, and its ownership and control will matter less than it does today. Information will be the key thing that flows between us and machines, using whatever device and technology is appropriate, and it is in this area that we see developments that are just over the horizon.

It may begin with simple things and small steps: if I have difficulty standing, my smartphone might alert a room guide who offers a chair, or it might alter my tour route or its timing. If I am prepared to share my profile then a venue could adapt to my time available, specialist interests, cultural values etc. We can thus begin to imagine heritage venues that will be able to deliver interpretation that is responsive to both your location and to your personal profile.

Key Knowledge — Location and Proximity Triggering

Multiple technologies can triggered content according to position or proximity.

All the trigger technologies are low-cost.

Multiple technologies can be used as they are not exclusive.

Only consider GPS solutions for outdoor scenarios where good satellite signals are likely to be received.

QR Codes and NFC tags will work both outdoors and indoors.

QR Codes and NFC tags are passive in that they rely on the user to scan the code or tag.

Bluetooth Beacons and GPS are the only technologies that can proactively alert a user to a point of interest without needing any visible notification.

Bluetooth Beacons require batteries that need to be changed regularly, and will not work in freezing temperatures.

Some modern phones can tell their orientation in space, so can be used to navigate like a movable window.

Visitor device capabilities and settings may limit what technology is usable.

Accessibility, Inclusivity, and Mindfulness

The visitor's actual experience depends not only on the venue and its interpretive facilities, but also on the characteristics of the visitor. Visitors come with different levels of subject knowledge, different physical and mental abilities, they may speak different languages and have different cultural values and touchstones. It is a major challenge to consider all the likely variations, but it is a challenge that is worth addressing to the maximum extent that is practicable. It is easy to underestimate the extent of differences and to unconsciously design interpretation for ourselves.

The good news is that digital interpretation opens up many more possibilities for tailored or even bespoke interpretation than physical signs and labels. The economics of multi-purposing and adapting are also very much better in the digital world. Even so, the list of considerations usually has to be prioritised, otherwise it has a tendency to grow and become unmanageable. The highest priority should be to ensure that no-one is completely excluded from having an interpretive experience of some form.

The terminology that is used in this area has been subject to considerable change over time. While this reflects a positive wish to be sympathetic and understanding, it can cause a degree of vagueness and verbal clumsiness in an attempt to re-define or remove stigmatising labels. We have used 'accessibility' to describe ways of overcoming 'disability', which we consider to be where people do not have a commonly held ability. We have used 'inclusiveness' to describe ways of meeting the challenge of the common variations found in every group of people. Finally, we have introduced the relatively new expression 'mindfulness' to describe the directing of human 'attention' that is so important as a part of understanding and learning. We think that this is a useful way to divide up the concepts involved. We accept that the terminology used may change and apologise should we offend anyone by the terms we have chosen.

Accessibility

Disabled people need to live as normal a life as possible, sharing the things that their friends and family do. Lack of consideration for such needs is morally unacceptable, and could constitute illegal discrimination. Separate provision for disability may sometimes be the only practicable option, although it is always less than satisfactory as it can make the disability more overt and lead to the disabled person feeling that they are the cause of inconvenience.

Undoubtedly the best approach is to design or adapt whatever is normal for the able-bodied, so that it can be used by people with a wide range of disabilities. Where this is not possible then special provision, made as convenient and low-key as possible, is a fall-back. Applying these principles to digital visitor information and interpretation, it is best to provide one facility for all, rather than building separate content or access methods 'for the disabled'.

There are many important insights to be gained by talking with any experts on this subject area, or directly with people that have specific challenges. Do make full use of your staff, volunteers, members and friends, as some of them are likely to have knowledge and contacts in this area and be motivated to help.

While ambulatory disability is not the only consideration, it tends to feature large in most heritage development projects. In some cases the very nature of heritage sites and buildings, and any protected legal status, precludes altering them to accommodate wheelchair access. In that case a digital substitute, while far short of ideal, has the potential to avoid complete exclusion.

Accessibility techniques

Follow technical standards

Use of standards is fundamental to both accessibility and inclusivity. The success of the Internet is largely down to the widespread adoption of standards that specify how text, images and other media should be presented for consumption by users. Other building blocks are the standards that define how that information is stored, searched and transmitted to the software used on computers, tablets and smartphones. Most of the standards relating to digital accessibility are Open Source and intended to be freely used by all. Closed and proprietary standards also exist that may appear to do the same or better, but they tend to lock users into specific hardware or software. In 100 years time, content encoded using widely used open standards are far more likely to be accessible by the devices of that era, than that encoded using formats used for short-term competitive advantage by a company that may no longer exist.

The standards for the Internet, including those that relate to accessibility, are maintained by a body known as the W3C at https://www.w3.org/. The consortium is literally open to all, and you will find invitations for you, as a member of the public, to contribute to the development of web standards. We cannot over-emphasise the advantages, in terms of cost and longevity, as well as accessibility, of keeping within open and widely adopted standards, both in buying from vendors and in developing any interpretive technology. Web sites are easily checked for accessibility using software tools and can be rated A, AA, or AAA according to how comprehensively they meet the W3C accessibility guidelines. While AAA is obviously the top rating, meeting it can restrict some of the functionality and the options you have, so many organisations aim for AA.

Screen readers

To serve sight-impaired users you should understand the use of image 'alt' tags. These are text descriptions of images so that 'screen reader' software can aurally provide that alternative information to their users about photographs, maps, and diagrams that they can't see. Most visually impaired users are likely to have a screen reader on their own device - another advantage of BYOD. The one point to note is that such aids only work if the content conforms with accessibility standards. For example, Content Management Systems can make provision for image 'alt' tags, but these will be useless if you upload an image but don't populate the alt fields with an adequate text description.

Subtitles and sign-language videos

Subtitles can help the many 'hard-of-hearing' visitors, especially in noisy environments. Hearing deteriorates naturally with age and sometimes through occupational exposure to noise. Certain frequencies tend to be lost first, which can make speech unintelligible in the presence of conflicting sounds of other frequencies.

Subtitles are of limited use to those who have been profoundly deaf from birth, as it is more difficult for them to acquire a reading ability, in which case alternative videos featuring sign language could be the only way to make a video accessible. You should be aware that, as with spoken language, sign languages vary around the world and even have regional accents. There is thus no one solution that fits all, but you might do some research and look to cater for the hearing-impaired among your primary audience demographic.

Virtual visits

For ambulatory disabilities, virtual visits by means of information pages and images, or better still the same audio or video tour enjoyed by the able-bodied, is a reasonable substitute if physical access is impracticable. Any virtual tour should take into consideration those who cannot do the physical tour. It could, for example, incorporate audio or video of any dynamic elements such as the sound or sight of working equipment. This is 'alternative provision' is potentially an acceptable means of accessibility compliance when applying to funding bodies for financial support.

Live webcam feeds

By utilising live webcams, anyone left out of a physical visit could be enabled to to follow their group step by step and so 'share' in the visit experience as far as is practicable through their BYOD or a loaned tablet. This opens up the possibility that the user can synchronise the process of their virtual visit with the physical visit of their group, so that there is a feeling of togetherness. A further idea is that direct verbal contact could be maintained by mobile phone, or even a teleconference.

Presentation options

Digital technology has the benefit over physical artefacts in that the content and presentation can be controlled separately. This means that you can present the same content in many visually different ways, which may be more appropriate for those with visual or mental incapacities. High contrast can make life easier for poor eyesight, while the avoidance of contrast and strobing is safer for those with epilepsy. Big buttons help those with arthritis or limited dexterity.

This separation between content and presentation, although not especially new, is not easy to understand if you have been used to laying out documents with a pen and paper, or even on a word processor, where layout is often hard coded by the author. Web pages are written in the language known as HTML (Hyper-Text Mark-up Language), which 'tags' blocks of content to classify them as a 'type'. Separate code written in a language called CSS (Cascading Style Sheets) defines how each 'type' will appear. Changing the CSS enables you to display the identical content in a completely different way. There is an online resource called 'Zen Garden' that promotes this at:

http://www.csszengarden.com

Content options

Society is increasingly understanding how mental health varies widely and the need to focus on what people can achieve rather than what they cannot. As more people are living with mental disabilities in the community, heritage interpretation needs to address what can be communicated and how best to do it so that aspects of interpretation that can be appreciated are not put beyond the reach of such visitors. Using digital technology, alternative selections and forms of content can be constructed that are aimed at different forms of concentration, reading ability or stimulation.

Inclusivity

The concept of 'Inclusivity' goes a step further than 'accessibility' in the sense of trying to provide experiences that everyone can get the best possible outcome from. It recognises that there is no such thing as the 'normal' or 'average' person - we are each a unique blend of skills, abilities and traits. This means that relatively subtle differences can create barriers. Age (at both ends of the scale), computer literacy, language, cultural values: there is a long list of things that can be a barrier to understanding. Exclusion can be partial: the material as presented simply does not 'click' or engage with the visitor. It also tends to be insidious, as the barriers tend to be less visible than those of disability.

When providing information by digital means there is the added potential to 'technologically exclude' those who do not have access to specific equipment, such as BYOD smartphones or tablets, or do not have the ability or manual dexterity to operate the provided equipment.

A new and insidious form of 'digital exclusion' in the heritage sector is the use of native apps (ie. apps developed specifically for iPhone and/or Android). This excludes those visitors who do not possess the specific type of device that is catered for (eg. Blackberry and Windows users). The reported popularity of particular makes and operating systems at any one time can be misleading. The media headlines tend to focus on current sales, rather than the base of installed devices. There will always be a substantial population who use older systems. As the number of smartphones in use is only just enough for half the world's population to own one each, the market is still open for new entrants, particularly in the populous and economically emerging continents, who may well 'leapfrog' the technological stages and infrastructures of the developed nations. The technology of mobile devices anyway changes rapidly, so it is unlikely that the popular platforms of today will be those of the future.

Inclusivity techniques

Follow technical standards

We make no apology for repeating this advice from the accessibility section. It really is important, particularly to avoid accidentally creating your own 'digital exclusion' through inappropriate choices, such as proprietary technology or native apps, for essential components of your interpretation.

BYOD user aids

A spin-off advantage of using BYOD as mainstream, or at least providing a BYOD option, is that the user is likely to have any aids that they need installed on their own device. This would be a difficult situation to achieve with hand-held or kiosk devices, as you would need to cater for multiple types of disability, whereas the person BYOD owner will have precisely met their own needs.

Multi-lingual

Such provision is a legal requirement in many bi-lingual regions of the world. Multiple languages are best facilitated by using authoring systems that come with a multi-lingual capability.This enables you to provide the same content in any number of languages. The user can switch between them at the touch of an on-screen button. The alternative is to structure your navigation to take languages into account. This is perhaps more appropriate if only some content is in another language, but generally makes the creation and management of multi-lingual content more complex.

Digital literacy

While this is a slowly lessening problem, some people do not know how to work digital devices and may even be afraid of touching them in case they break it. While the young are generally highly literate in this respect, some may misuse learned methods such as 'pinch-to-zoom' on touch screen kiosks that only support on-screen buttons. Catering for all the common alternatives is better than expecting a visitor to follow instructions. Obviousness and consistency within the device should be a part of navigation design. Consistency with common devices is desirable.

Digital literacy is not just age-related, but tends to be more a product of the extent to which the older generation's working life brought them into contact with digital technology as it emerged. Remember that Bill Gates (MicroSoft), Steve Jobs (Apple), and Sir Tim Berners-Lee (inventor of the Web) were all born in 1955 - as were the authors!

Equipment availability

A drawback of BYOD is that some will always be lacking the equipment, or maybe the battery power remaining, to use their own device. It is important to provide alternatives. Low-cost touch-screen tablets can be installed as permanent public 'kiosk' devices at key locations. Such tablets can be locked down by special kiosk software to prevent misuse and interference. An alternative to fixed point kiosks would be a supply of loan or rental tablets that the visitor could carry around.

Navigation options

Visitor subject knowledge varies enormously from the expert to the not-interested. Giving the visitor clear choices in terms of the route that they follow through your content, and the depth to which they go, will help each visitor to get what is appropriate for them. This is not to say that you should not challenge or surprise, but that you should, for example, give the option to say 'I've had enough of this bit' and skip sections. It is not easy when time and effort have gone into creating interpretive material, but letting them chose to move on is better than losing the visitor altogether.

Webcams

While we have a dedicated chapter for webcams, the concept of inclusivity might also be extended to using webcams to make available material that cannot otherwise easily be shown to members of the public, and so would normally be reserved for the qualified elite. For example living organisms under a microscope, nesting sites where public access would risk disturbance, or places that are physically too small or too dangerous to give public access.

Webcams can also be used to make interesting activity watchable where it is unlikely to be in progress during a visit: an example would be automatically generated highlights of the activity of nocturnal wildlife, perhaps made visible by thermal or infrared imaging; or time-lapse used to record a slow process, such as restoration or eggs hatching.

Mindfulness

In his seminal work on interpretation, Freeman Tilden argues that interpretation is a means to enable the visitor to understand a historical or natural heritage site, and hence to appreciate and to value it, which in turn leads to support for its protection and conservation. While the digitisation of interpretation could be seen as simply offering a modern method for delivering these fundamental principles, there is a contrary view. The distraction and immersive nature of our digital media could lead to visitors burying their heads in our virtual world and failing to appreciate the real one around them. In a crowd of visitors in a quiet place, the noise from several soundtracks, each at a different point in a narrative, and perhaps being played in multiple languages, could be a severe distraction.

There are some concerns that that young people are growing up to be dependent on smartphones, and that their minds are increasingly absent from the real world for large parts of the time. We would argue that negative views of the effects of technological change on young minds have been put forward by each successive generation - from pop and jazz music on the radio and children watching too much TV, to computer games and social media. Such fears have only ever partially been vindicated, as the human mind seems to have a remarkable ability to adapt to what it grows up with. While there are accidents due to the distraction of mobile phones, causing changes in the law for drivers, and some embarrassing clips on social media, the nature of the fears expressed are largely those of the generation for whom the technology is new and perhaps is more disruptive.

Having said that, in the context of interpretation, the objective is to appreciate and enjoy the place being visited. It is possible to get carried away by the exciting possibilities and in the process to let the medium become the message. Even when this is not the case, it is still possible that the message can dominate the 'sense of place' that is one of the primary objectives of heritage interpretation. We consider that such failings are mostly due to interpretation design rather than a product of the technology used. The intelligent designer can select appropriate media; they can create periods of explanation followed by periods of appreciation - silent appreciation if that is best. We perhaps need to develop more skill in the psychology of storytelling using digital media, rather than blame the media themselves. It may be that the greatest challenge for interpreters today is to develop digital content that can hold the attention when it needs to, but at the same time makes the individual more mindful of their surroundings.

Key Knowledge — Accessibility, Inclusiveness and Mindfulness

Disabled accessibility is a legal requirement in many countries.

Make the disabled experience as close as possible to the standard experience.

Adopt standards, especially the Web accessibility standards maintained by the W3C.

Become knowledgeable about the different forms of impairments and the wide range of aids, such as screen readers, sign language, and subtitles.

Live webcams can be a fall-back 'substitute' where ambulatory accessibility is not practical.

'Inclusiveness' means not excluding people due to common factors such as age, technical competence, reading ability etc.

If you only making your content for some devices you will be creating 'digital exclusion'.

Use your staff, volunteers, friends, and members as a resource for understanding, designing and testing.

How we direct the visitor's attention and 'mindfulness' is a significant consideration when using inherently 'immersive' digital tools.

Remote, Outdoor and Unattended

Protect 8

The harshness of the outdoor environment, and the absence of staff and infrastructure, should not stop us from providing digital interpretation. Indeed the appreciation and impact of digital interpretation is somewhat enhanced by being available where the visitor least expects it. For outdoor and unattended environments we do need to think about the additional challenges and risks that they present, and the forms of protection that we can use.

Power

Environmental issues have driven significant recent improvements in battery and solar panel technology. The increased performance and availability, coupled with reduced cost, make solar power a viable option for most electronics. A spin-off advantage is that they do not involve potentially lethal voltages and so the precautions that are required with mains power are absent. Low-voltage current-limited supplies can also be made intrinsically fire safe by restricting the energy available to create a source of ignition.

Solar power

It is a common misconception that the solar panels are the only system component in solar power. This is not practical due to their fluctuating output in response to the widely varying outdoor light levels. Instead, a solar panel is used to keep a battery charged and the battery provides the steady power source. Between the solar panel and the battery is an electronic gadget called a 'charge controller', to which your device is also connected. The charge controller is responsible for adjusting where the power is coming from and where it goes to in order to optimise the power and life of all three components - the solar panel, the battery, and your electronics (known as the 'load').

There are a number of important considerations with solar power that are not commonly known. The first is that, despite the name 'solar', they do not need direct sunlight. They simply need enough light to work, which normally means a good view of the sky. The second is the effect of shadows and debris. It is a natural assumption that if, say, 10% of a panel becomes covered then you expect to lose 10% of the power. This assumption is completely wrong. A solar panel is made up of individual cells, connected together in series to make a chain. If just one of the cells becomes deeply shaded or malfunctions, then it effectively breaks the chain and little or no electricity will flow. For this reason it is important to site a panel where it has a consistent and even exposure to light from the sky.

Solar panels and their accompanying batteries involve electro-chemical reactions and these will degrade in extremes of temperature and over time. We recommend an annual maintenance check involving a panel clean at least every year, replacing the battery in line with the manufacturer's recommendation - in the case of 12v lead-acid 'leisure' batteries (not car 'starter' batteries, which look the same) commonly associated with solar power, every two years would be reasonable.

Although you can calculate or measure the power requirements of your equipment, there will be a deterioration in performance of your solar panels and battery equipment over time. Combined with the tendency for vendors to publish only their best obtainable performance figures, it means that it is always necessary to apparently over-specify an installation in terms of power, so that it will continue to work over the long-term. Given the several factors, none of which are precisely known, a 'rule of thumb' that we recommend is to over-specifythe calculated power by a blanket factor of 10x.

Weather

Even fairly innocuous weather is generally harsh for any man-made article. From the bleaching effect of the sun to the splitting power of freezing water, we have to anticipate a degree of deterioration over time of the enclosures that we use to house equipment. However, the electronics can be kept relatively trouble-free by understanding the threats and by taking simple protection and mitigation measures.

A comprehensive approach for extreme environments is to layer several protective 'shells' with each doing a specific job - the inner one a dust-filtered, insect-proofed enclosure, the middle one a larger 'stable volume' with an impervious material but a small drain/vent hole at the bottom, then an outer 'weather shelter' just to add protection from direct sun, ice or snow. Inevitably some situations will involve a compromise, and the optimum will depend upon the local climate.

Water

Water is a known enemy of electronics, as anyone who has dropped a phone down the toilet will tell you. For this reason most people's natural instinct is to try to provide a watertight seal, often to formal standards such as 'IP66'. This is the wrong approach. We have to remember that, as well as a liquid, water is always present in the air in the invisible gas form that we call humidity, and this humidity can condense into liquid water droplets - steam or dew - if the humidity rises, or the temperature or pressure drops - whether the environment is sealed or not.

Enclosures for electronics need to be 'weatherproof' but not 'waterproof', in the same way that a house resists weather but is not completely sealed, and your clothes are meant to be 'breathable' otherwise you will get perspiration build-up inside them. If you seal electronics in an airtight container then, unless you are able to do this in a perfectly dry atmosphere, condensation may form and you will have liquid water trapped in your sealed container. Airtight sealing prevents ventilation and that traps heat. Batteries can emit gases that are corrosive to electronics, so airtight sealing is again a bad idea.

Generally, electronics require 'shelter'. As water falls with gravity, a covering over the top that is waterproof, and vents that are sheltered from falling rain are often enough. If this weather shelter is added over the general enclosure that houses the equipment, the underlying electronics should be very safe.

The most challenging conditions are those found near the coast. Salt is corrosive to electronics, and the presence of salt mist and blown sand in the air makes it very difficult to protect electronics. Enclosures can have filtration that will help to condense out salt onto the filter material before it reaches the electronics. Electronic components can be close-sealed by the application of coatings to the circuit boards, or by 'potting' them in a block of resin compound. However, these approaches can compromise heat dissipation and can introduce their own technical problems, as well as making repair and replacement more difficult, so they are only worth using for extreme environments.

Cold

Batteries provide energy from chemical reactions and chemistry tends to stop working below freezing, so you have to anticipate failure under these conditions. This is clearly a major consideration for outdoor solar power and for beacon technology, both of which rely on batteries. You can to some extent insulate against short-term cold, such as overnight temperature dips. It helps if there is a heat source so that the insulation has some heat to keep contained. This might be achieved by locating electronics such that their slight heat helps keep the battery warm. You will though need to keep any corrosive battery gases away from the electronics.

There are some new capacitor technologies, known as 'ultra-caps' that will work at sub-zero temperatures. Capacitors work by storing electricity directly in a static form in thin plates. They are much more expensive than batteries, but are being used in high-value applications such as the automotive sector, where electronics have to work reliably in sub-zero temperatures.

Generally speaking, electronic components, including solar panels, work well in cold temperatures.

Heat

Heat shortens the life of almost all electronic components. As the temperature rises the lifetime shortens alarmingly - by as much as the 4th power. For this reason you should always provide adequate means of ventilation so that the amount of heat generated by the specific type of electronics can escape. In particular you should provide shade so that sunlight does not directly heat electronics or the enclosure that contains them.

Wildlife and livestock

Insects and animals like to find safe, warm, dry spaces, and so electronic enclosures can be naturally very attractive to them.

Sound and light can also attract specific species of insect in which case physical barriers are the only real preventative measure. Insect screens need to be of relatively fine mesh - ideally of some hard and non-corroding and non-degrading material such as stainless steel.

Animals are curious and will sniff and lick objects. Any firm objects are likely to be used as scratching aids. Livestock on farms are surprisingly destructive in this respect. The only real solution is to locate the objects out of reach.

Humans

If there is no-one around, then no equipment or facility is entirely safe. However, malicious acts are hard to perpetrate against something that you cannot see or touch. Hence the use of Wi-Fi and radio signals with BYOD means that the potential for harm can be easily reduced, and with some thought the potential can even be eliminated.

Theft

Systems based on common consumer electronics present a severe temptation as they have a known value, can be easily concealed, and are readily sold. The same applies to a lesser extent for re-saleable items such as batteries, solar panels, and anything containing valuable metals.

Tablets provided as fixed touch-screen kiosks can be installed behind strong protective panels so that they are not easy to steal. These can be made, and some vendors sell them.

Specialist equipment is less tempting as it does not have a ready market and its unusual nature makes it more conspicuous and identifiable. However, the average thief is not always logical.

Vandalism

Vandalism presents a more difficult challenge than theft as it has more complex motivations, and damage is often easier to achieve covertly than removal. Again, Wi-Fi and radio solutions provide the best answer. If there is necessarily some base station equipment it could be:

- Hidden, as the location that a signal is coming from is difficult to ascertain
- Secured, to make access difficult
- Out-of-reach, so that the potential vandal would need a ladder

Adding webcams to an installation would also help to deter any misbehaviour by recording evidence that is stored out of reach of the perpetrator. This can often be done with Wi-Fi webcams that are added to, or are even part of, the interpretation system.

Physical infrastructure

Where there is no existing built infrastructure mobile digital and BYOD offers the only workable solution. It is possible to install an independent internet/Wi-Fi unit within interpretation panels and power them with a solar installation. The entire system, including a solar panel, can be housed within a roofed information point design that can also offer seating or shelter.

Some sensitive sites have restrictions on digging, or making any kind of permanent installation, in which case the design may be able to incorporate a concrete pad, or a container base that can be filled with sand, so that its weight holds it in place. This has the advantage of being re-locatable which can be a requirement when interpreting environmental works that will change location over time.

Key Knowledge — Remote, Outdoor and Unattended

Interpretation is more appreciated where it is not usually available.

BYOD is often the only solution in these environments.

Solar power means that digital equipment can be used away from mains power.

Battery technology can be used for temporary 'open day' events.

Don't seal electronic equipment - weatherproof it.

Protect equipment from heat, precipitation, insects, animals and humans.

Phone and Wi-Fi signals

9

Most of us will know that 'wireless' or 'radio' is a way that we can transmit digital data without wires using an invisible part of the electro-magnetic spectrum. Mobile phones, bluetooth, Wi-Fi, cordless phones, TV and radio etc. all make use of the 'radio' part of this spectrum to communicate to devices. The visible part of the electro-magnetic spectrum we see as light, and the radio waves that we are concerned with behave in ways similar to light - for example, travelling in straight lines (called 'line-of-sight') and being absorbed by some materials and reflected by others - so it is often useful to image them as light, and the aerial or antenna as a light bulb.

The different bits of the radio spectrum are distinguished by their wavelength or frequency. 'Frequency' is the more common way of expressing the radio bit of the spectrum. So technologies like Wi-Fi and Bluetooth are each allocated some bunches of frequencies that they can use, which are usually called 'bands'. For example, Wi-Fi can operate anywhere in the world, without any licence, provided it uses the 2.4 GigaHertz or 5 GigaHertz frequency bands. Mobile phone services use a different set of frequencies. Your mobile phone may or may not work in countries around the world, depending on whether it is capable of using the local frequency bands, of which there are several, that have been licenced to the phone service providers.

Within the bands there are specific frequencies defined as channels. Only one device can be using a channel at any moment in time. However, as data is transmitted in short bursts, channels can be time-shared by a number of devices by giving them a way of synchronising so that they do not interfere with each other's transmissions.

What affects radio signals?

As the radio frequencies that we are concerned with are 'line-of-sight' they are not good at going around things, and will be weakened ('attenuated' in techno-speak) by passing through objects such as walls and trees.

Radio waves travel best when there is nothing in the way, so positioning an antenna high up is usually best. Even so, they will gradually weaken over distance, just like a light beam. The 'range' of a signal is not a sudden cut-off, but more a gradual fading to a point where it is not usable by the 'average' device.

The quality of the transmitting and receiving antennas is important. However, we all want our mobile phones to be small and not to have aerials sticking out of them. This means that the 'average' mobile device involves a compromise between radio performance and convenience. This in turn means that some devices will work better than others, depending on their internal antenna design, and even on how you are holding them in terms of orientation, and the signal going through your hand and body.

Mobile Phone Services

How it works

Modern phones digitise everything before they send it. This has the advantage thatboth voice and data can be transmitted via the same signal. Each phone looks for a nearby transmitter and, providing it has a valid account, connects into the phone provider's network from where the digitised voice and data is carried to its destination, potentially using other phone networks and the Internet to get there.

Range

Phones time-share a channel by a process that gives each device a pre-determined time slot. This means that as a device gets further away from a transmitter mast there comes a point where the time taken for radio waves to make the round trip means that it misses part of its slot, and the service degrades, which means it will slow down. The full capability of a signal is only achievable for 5 Km from the transmitting mast and gradually reduces unit, by a maximum range of 35 Km, it will not work at all. The data portion of the service suffers more than the voice and text part, so although a mast may offer 3G or 4G for example, the actual browsing experience may be unusably slow, especially for streaming rich media files such as video.

Limitations

For a mobile phone to be a practical method of connecting to all your visitors you will need a good signal from all the national service providers to be present. Each mobile provider runs their own transmitter masts and coverage is part of their competitive offering, so they do not readily share. The exception is when 'roaming' in another country. The 'home' operators often have agreements with several local 'remote' operators to carry their calls. However, roaming charges have historically been extremely expensive and, although there are efforts in some countries to regulate perceived over-charging, users are often unwilling to use their phone while roaming. Some experienced travellers may even purchase local pay-as-you-go SIM cards to get reasonable rate calls during their stay.

Phone price plans vary enormously and, while some may be on unlimited data plans, others will be pay-as-you-go, or have plan limits. Charges for going beyond those limits are normally punitive. The normal pattern of a user's data usage may be drastically increased if they work their way through many videos during a heritage visit.

There is a further issue of reliability in that phone providers can move their transmitters, and sometimes do in order to reduce land and lower rental costs. Overall we advise that, other than at some locations in major cities, mobile phone signal is not suitable for heritage interpretation.

Wi-Fi Connections

How it works

Wi-Fi uses a set of unlicensed radio channels that are reserved specifically for Wi-Fi. Any user can set up a low power transmitter - such as your Wi-Fi hub or base station at home.

Wi-Fi channels time-share by using the internet system of only one device 'speaking' at once, and others waiting for a gap to speak - rather like a polite dinner-table conversation. The digitised information is split up into 'packets' that are addressed to a destination, just like a letter is addressed before you drop it into the postal system. Each device listens for and collects those packets of information that are addressed to it, and re-assembles them back into whatever was transmitted - a page of information, an audio or video file, etc.

There are currently two bands of channels in use. One is on the 'traditional' 2.4 GHz band, which is currently the most common, so is often crowded in urban environments. The other is on the 'new' 5 GHz band, which is less used and also has more space, so is less crowded and less likely to suffer from interference.

The 2.4 GHz band consists in theory of either 11 or 14 channels, depending on the country, but in practice the channels overlap, so normally only the three channels designated 1, 6 and 11 (and in some countries 14) are used in order to prevent interference (see below). The 5 GHz band has around 19 channels, depending on local regulations, and they do not overlap, so there is room for many more devices to communicate simultaneously in crowded urban environments.

The drawback of 2.4 GHz is that it can become seriously overcrowded in urban situations such as flats or shared office accommodation, where there are lots of heavy users. The drawback of 5 GHz is that the higher frequency does not carry as far and is more easily stopped or weakened by objects.

Range

As the power of Wi-Fi is limited by law, its range is limited to the immediate vicinity. Having said that, the type of antenna used on both the transmitter and the receiver makes a big difference. This is because the transmitter signal and the receiver sensitivity can be concentrated by the antenna so as to be more intense in a specific pattern. By choosing an antenna that suits your type of environment you will achieve optimum results.

The Wi-Fi signal can also be thought of as falling to earth a bit like a jet of water would under gravity if you sprayed it horizontally. The higher you site the antenna, the longer the signal can travel before it hits the ground. Placing an antenna on or near the ground will dramatically shorten the range.

Obstructions

The ideal is to have nothing but clear air 'line-of-sight' between the transmitter antenna and the user. In the real world we need to use enclosures for hiding and securing Wi-Fi transmitters. Plastic, wood and glass are virtually radio-transparent, so are good materials to use. Bear in mind that it is the antenna that counts, and not the electronics. Extension cables enable the placing of an antenna several metres away from the electronics.

Walls will weaken (attenuate) the signal. How much they do this depends on the material they are made of, how thick they are, and how damp they are. Water molecules absorb radio waves, so damp walls, trees in leaf, and people, are all things that contain a lot of water. With so many variables, testing on-site is really the only way to be sure how well a signal will cope with obstructions.

Reflections

Metal and metallised surfaces, such as mirrors, reflect radiowaves. This means that virtually none will pass through. However, the reflected signal is a useful thing. In a steel-clad building, such as many transport museums have, one transmitter is often enough to fill a large hall. It often does not matter where it is placed, even if there are objects obstructing the line-of-sight. The signal is bounced around the walls and seems to be present everywhere.

Keep in mind that complex reflections can degrade the quality of the signal, so it may be strong but less able to carry data. Some causes of reflections can be metal objects such as cabinets, cars, or cookers. Even the thermal insulation hidden in the roof, walls, and floor of a building may have a foil layer that is radio-reflective. Some U/V window coatings and some metallic paints can create a thin but reflective metal layer.

Reflectors can be useful in order to prevent radio waves being absorbed into damp walls. Even a mirror-tile or a thin sheet of aluminium baking foil will act as a reflector, and can be hidden on the back of a mounting board, where it will still be effective. Tests have shown that the line-of-sight signal in front of a damp wall is 4x stronger with a reflector.

Although water itself absorbs Wi-Fi radio waves, the surface of water, such as a lake, will act as a reflector at a shallow angle.

Interference

The Wi-Fi radio bands are very close to those of other devices, including cordless phones, bluetooth, radar, and microwave ovens. While they should not in principle interfere with each other, extreme proximity, poor set-up, or faulty equipment means that interference is possible, and is difficult to identify, as it is coming from a non-Wi-Fi source that will not be listed as present.

Within the 2.4 GHz band other Wi-Fi installations on immediately adjacent channels will cause more interference that other Wi-Fi on the same channel. This is because those transmitting and listening on the same channel respect the 'one at a time' principle, whereas devices on adjacent channels are not aware of each other and so can talk over each other's transmissions. These clashes mean that one or both has to re-send their spoiled data packets, which slows down the process far more dramatically than controlled sharing of a channel.

Understanding speed, quality and overload

We have all experienced glitches in broadcast media due to signal failures, interference and the like. Given that Wi-Fi is a shared radio channel that is carrying digitised data, and given that there are a lot of factors that affect the quality of the channel, it is logical that it will encounter glitches. The Internet protocols that Wi-Fi uses are very good at recovering from glitches and most of the time we do not notice them. Maybe a web page takes a bit longer to load, but that is not serious. With real-time media, such as audio and video, smooth continuity is paramount or it becomes an unacceptable experience. There are two factors that prevent glitches. One is the quality of the signal. The other is the amount of data that we try to transfer in a given time.

To understand what happens when a glitch occurs and how to minimise them, it is necessary to grasp the basics of how the internet sends data. A useful analogy is the postal service. Your content is divided up into postage-sized packets, each one is addressed, and dropped into the system. It is routed to its destination by having the address read at each point in its journey. Finally the received packets are opened and assembled by the recipient.

Now, let's suppose that we (or other postal users) overload the poor postie so that their vehicle is stuffed full, and they drop and lose packets in the street on their way to making deliveries. Once the missing packets are identified by the receiver they have to ask the sender to re-send them, which takes time. If it does not matter what order the packets arrive in, then a delay caused to some packets may not be serious. If, however the content of the packets is time sensitive - let's say that each is one instalment of a day-by-day TV listings magazine - then if it does not arrive on time it is useless.

If our digital system loses packets of data that belong in a video and the replacement packets do not arrive in time, then the video stops. We either need to get our postie a bigger vehicle, or send less cumbersome packets. Wi-Fi is a known as a 'lossy' method of communication, because of interference and potential packet 'collisions' - it is a bit of a careless postie - and so we have to keep not only within its theoretical bandwidth, but also allow some space for re-sends of lost packets. Re-sends will be greater if we have a poor signal and also if we try to send too many packets at once. The digital equivalent is trying to send files that are very big, or super high-quality real-time media at high bit rates, since this overloads our Wi-Fi postie, who will lose more packets. If your audio or video tends to 'stutter' or 'buffer', particularly when further away from your Wi-Fi range, reduce the bit-rate, which is a measure of the volume of packets. This may be possible without compromising quality, although there is a minimum bit-rate for each level of screen size and quality.

Satellite Communication

Contrary to popular belief, around 99% of the world's international point-to-point data communications go via cables rather than satellite - including phone calls, texts, and internet traffic. While satellites are used for 'one-to-many' applications such as TV broadcasting, the cost of satellites has so far made it uneconomic for everyday point-to-point communication, except in extreme situations where there is no alternative. It is not only the cost of construction and launch, but the need for a lot of electrical power for relaying high volumes of data, with only a limited amount of solar power available. In addition, the time taken by radio waves to make the 70,000km round trip to a geostationary satellite causes a half-second delay, which introduces an unacceptable latency into many applications.

There are developments in progress to provide satellite-based Wi-Fi internet connectivity for passengers on aircraft. This is a high-value application that will only provide connectivity to the relatively small number of people airborne at any one time - and they will have to pay.

While the use of satellites will undoubtedly become more widespread and cheaper over time, unless a breakthrough technology changes the situation, the idea that satellite technology can solve the world's internet connectivity problems is, at present at least, unrealistic.

Key Knowledge — Phone and Wi-Fi signals

Mobile phones, Wi-Fi, NFC, and Bluetooth are all radio technologies that are used to communicate wirelessly with mobile devices.

To be usable for interpretation, phone signals from all the providers would have to be present, in sufficient strength and quality to carry data for many users. This is often not the case at heritage sites that are away from centres of population.

A Wi-Fi antenna can realistically cover a circle of up to to 500 m diameter and handle up to 40 simultaneous users. Multiple Wi-Fi hotspots or a contiguous network can cover much bigger areas.

Radio travels in straight lines like light, and can be blocked or reflected by different materials. Radio-transparent materials are: plastic, glass, and (dry) wood. Radio-absorbing materials are: thick walls, damp walls or earth, trees in leaf. Radio-reflecting materials are: metals, including thin aluminium foils used in insulation.

Wi-Fi operates in the 2.5 GHz or 5 GHz bands, and can suffer interference from other sources operating in those bands. Common 2.4 GHz sources include cordless phones and microwave ovens, as well as other Wi-Fi transmitters.

The way you format your content will have a big effect on how fast and reliably it works over a radio connection. (see chapter on Working with Media)

Many people wrongly believe that satellites are the basis of digital communication rather than the ground-based infrastructure.

Standards and Intellectual Property

10

Standards is a slightly abstract concept, but a very important one in the digital world. It applies right across hardware, software and systems, so it is useful to have a grasp of the general concepts and effects in order to manage the way that they impact your digital interpretation.

Although we use the word 'standards' in many ways and contexts, what we mean here is the agreed way of doing something. For example, we all drive on either the left or the right depending on which country we are in. Which side of the road is chosen does not matter as much as the fact that we all follow the same rule, and it is public knowledge. To extend the analogy, in order to illustrate the imperfections in standards, the driving standard is not global. If it was, life would be easier for drivers and for vehicle manufacturers. However, by simply being told 'this country drives on the left/right' we know what to do and can live with the two standards. Without any standard, driving would be confusing, and somewhat dangerous.

If we want to connect equipment together, or to run a software on a particular hardware, or put existing content onto a new device, having good standards is what enables us to do this. Standards may also specify the minimum performance that has to be achieved in terms of power, speed etc. In fact, standards in digital technology have to define a lot of technical parameters. Thismeans a lot of work co-ordinating all the stakeholders, as some choices may favour one product over another, and some choices may make for better or worse performance. The issues of performance, innovation, ownership, lock-in, and competitive advantage all tend to pull standards in different directions. However, for us as the end user, standards would be:

- Make things interoperable
- Protect you from vendor lock-in
- Establish performance levels

Standards also have a dark side. Control or domination of standards can be profitable. Standards can also be used as a tool to exclude and restrict, as in Digital Rights Management (DRM).

IPR

Intellectual Property Rights (IPR) - sometimes called 'copyright' although that is only a part of IPR - were created to give artists, inventors, and innovators the ability to profit from their work by giving them a limited right to a monopoly. IPR is the subject of much debate, as some feel that they in fact restrict innovation and give big organisations a legal tool to stifle small competitors to the disadvantage of the public.

In the digital age, copying is so easy, and can take on new forms, such as 'pulling' content on-the-fly from original sources, that there has been an explosion of issues, and the legal and moral codes have often lagged behind the new practices.

IPR is thus a large and complex subject, often misinterpreted by the public, and the rules vary around the world. We will restrict ourselves here to the aspects that are relevant to managing mobile digital interpretation.

Types of standard

Proprietary Standards

These are 'standards' designed and implemented by one or more manufacturers or vendors. They tend to emerge in very early-stage technologies as the vendor has had to design the technology from scratch, and make all the elements and system components. While it is clearly risky to be locked into a vendor's technology and their commercial fortunes, sometimes it is the only option if you want the end result.

Cost and risk are the price that so-called 'early-adopters' have to pay for having the latest and the coolest technology. A less exciting, but more wise approach, is to be part of the 'second wave' adopters that buy into a technology once it has stabilised, which is often evidenced by the emergence of clear and common 'de facto' or 'de jure' standards.

'De Facto' Standards

This term refers to standards that emerge from widespread use. They may follow on from the commercial success of a proprietary standard, or emerge from a popular way of doing something. It can lead to problems if the standard originated as proprietary, and the owner then tries to monetise their now widely used intellectual property.

'De Jure' Standards

Some standards are designed and governed by international bodies. One good example is the Internet, which derives its many standards from the W3C consortium. This ensures world-wide interoperability of hardware and applications and underpinned the success of the Internet and the Web.

These 'official' standards are sometimes known as 'de jure' standards, meaning that they are arrived at by an open and quasi-legal process, and are to some extent enforced by co-operation. The main benefit of such standards are universal interoperability, and protecting users from lock-in by vendors.

Types of IPR

Copyright

Most sovereign states have laws that to some extent or other prevent the commercial exploitation of the intellectual work of another person. Some of these laws, such as patents and copyrights, are then incorporated into international trade agreements. The subject is a complex one, but some basic features are fairly universal, certainly in the Western world.

Before using any digital material that you did not create, you should do some research on the material itself, and on the legal environment of the intended use, in order to be sure that you understand and document the legal basis on which you will use it. There can be a tendency to be over-cautious of the legal implications, and many scenarios that could potentially expose you to litigation are unlikely to end in court because no civil harm has been done. IPR laws and agreements create 'civil' offences, meaning that it is something that the person you harm has to sue for. They are not 'criminal' offences that law enforcement agencies monitor. Generally speaking your actions need to do economic harm to someone's livelihood in order to give a person or organisation the motivation and the practical possibility of suing in court. Low-level and non-commercial use is thus not likely to be an issue. Legal action on IPR is mostly an issue where significant money or high profile is involved. Having said that, it is polite and civilised, as well as legally wise, to take reasonable steps to seek and record the author's permission for anything that you want to copy or re-use.

Open Source

Many hardware designs, and software programs are now available as 'Open Source'. The fundamental advantage of Open Source comes if you want to adapt, or interface to, an item. Once hardware is built, or software 'compiled' into a runtime version, it may be impossible to understand how it works.

Taken literally, Open Source simply means that a programmer's source code or an engineer's design is published, and legal restrictions may still apply to copying and using it. In practice, most Open Source products are free to use and adapt. Open Source has the advantage that anyone can design other system components to work with the item. If the licence permits you can improve or extend it and re-publish your work to an Open Source community of users who may take it further. This has given rise to a new dynamic of collective software creation and maintenance by a community of user/developers. With an Open Source product you cannot in theory be left stranded by any action of the proprietor, because you have the option to understand how it works and to re-engineer it.

Creative Commons

Many creative and artistic works are available under one of the 'Creative Commons' licences, sometimes called 'copyleft'. The word 'commons' is used in the sense that parcels of agricultural land were once available for use by anyone in a community. A Creative Commons licence broadly means that anyone can use the work for free, but again attention is needed to the type of licence. Some have specific restrictions in terms of commercial use, attribution, changing the item, or incorporating it in anything else, so you do need to examine and understand the licence terms.

Fortunately Creative Commons licence terms follow a standard, rather than being specified individually, so it is easy to look them up and understand them. They are usually represented by a code - for example CC BY-SA Attribution-ShareAlike. Each code has both a full legal description, a simple plain-language description, and a machine-readable code that can be included as metadata. By licensing your own work under Creative Commons you can automatically give others a clear permission, within limits, as to how they may use your work.

Device Locking

Digital Rights Management

In recent years the imposition of Digital Rights Management (DRM) has been the major publishers response to widespread private and commercial copying and 'pirating'. This may lock commercially published content to specific hardware, or world region. Content may only be playable on devices that support DRM. This is obviously a potential problem for interpretation that wants to draw on widely published content, as even if you obtain the publisher's permission, DRM technology may block it. It affects mostly high-value entertainment content downloaded or installed on a device, so does not affect BYOD.

Online Store Locks

Some mobile device manufacturers, most notably Apple, lock their devices to prevent them downloading media or apps other than from their official online 'stores'. This helps them to prevent users downloading viruses and unsuitable content. It also enables them to monetise apps and content by being the payment gatekeeper.

These restrictions mean that, while a BYOD user may play a video or use a web app their device will refuse to download it. It also means that kiosk and loan devices need to keep within published apps and media, or be re-engineered to break the lock - a process known as 'jailbreaking'.

Organisational locking

A few large organisations lock their corporate devices (generally Windows Operating System) to restrict them to limited network access. This now uncommon, and is perhaps becoming less so as personal devices and internet access become ubiquitous.

Key Knowledge — Standards and Intellectual Property

Standards enable interoperability and help to prevent obsolescence and vendor lock-in.

Several flavours of standard co-exist, each with different characteristics and effects.

Many 'de jure' standards such as web and internet standards have global consortia that develop and maintain them collaboratively - such as the W3C.

Intellectual Property is a generic term covering patents and copyrights - a legal concept that applies to the digital world.

You should always seek permission of the creator, owner, or sponsor, and at least be clear about the basis on which you have a right to use someone else's artistic work.

Copyright gives the creator the right to a monopoly on exploitation for a fixed time.

Copyright infringement is a civil offence. If you do economic or reputational harm to someone by exploiting their work, they can sue you for the damage done. Most people are overly cautious about copyright in situations where money and malicious intent is not involved.

The growing trend towards 'Open Source' and 'Creative Commons' is to some extent moving us away from ownership and protection of IPR towards sharing and collaboration. There is an argument that this is more productive and beneficial for everyone.

Open Source and Creative Commons are not licence free. They have their own structure of licence options.

Widespread domestic copying and commercial pirating has led device makers and publishers to lock devices so that content cannot be downloaded, copied, or used, other than as intended - a process known as Digital Rights Management (DRM).

Some manufacturers have locked devices exclusively to their own online stores for the download of apps and rich media. This is ostensibly for user protection, but arguably also for commercial reasons.

A New Creative Toolbox   11

The most exciting thing about digital media is that it opens up new creative possibilities by radically extending the toolset that is available. While novel technology itself can be attractive, and is one way of refreshing your offering, novelty is, by definition, short lived, and is never going to be a substitute for well-designed interpretation. What digital does do is to open up a radically extended toolbox with which to design interpretation that is more engaging. This extended toolbox has the capability to be interactive, to be discreet, to reveal a narrative in a programmed sequence, to interact with the visitor to reflect their interests. If you only use the text and images, plus some audio and video, then you are not reaping the full fruits of the digital world.

There is always excited talk in the heritage media of cutting-edge possibilities, to the extent that the unrealistic hyperbole even becomes counter-productive. On the other hand, conservatism of usage tends to lag a long way behind what is realistically possible. Doing new things does mean taking risks, but those risks are as manageable as any other, and the potential reward is something unique and attractive.

You don't have to be cutting edge to produce exciting content. When demonstrating the digital content loaned to us by interpreters, we notice that some specific things seem to have had a magical effect on most people, and they are not especially difficult or cutting edge. We have come to describe these as the 'Wow!' factor items. We list here some ideas and suggestions from an interpretation viewpoint rather than a technological one in the hope that they will be a starting point for your own creative ideas that the technology can then support.

No Infrastructure - no problem

The daily frustrations of connectivity mean that the simple ability to use a smartphone to view information in a wild and remote place is impressive. Using native apps or a locally-generated internet that confers independence from connectivity means that the user can do just that, even in places where their smartphone has ceased to work as a phone. Giving people information while they sit in their car, or walk or cycle a trail, is disproportionately appreciated compared to the same facility in a big city museum, largely because it is so unexpected.

Integrate physical to web

Any printed leaflet, badge, sign, or other printed artefact can incorporate QR codes that link to web based content. This means that items on a map can have digital content associated with them and triggered by scanning the code, or inputting a short URL as an alternative. Signs can tell you about the place where you are standing, from simply locating you on a map, to an in-depth lesson on the geological, morphological, natural, and historical heritage of that spot.

A dedicated app can take this further, and interact with photographs on the printed page or an interpretation panel. There is an emerging concept of the 'Physical Web' and 'Internet of Things' that will see a gradual integration of our real and digital worlds. Future visitors will be quite used to moving seamlessly between the two.

Discreet Interpretation

For some venues, such as historic buildings and landscaped gardens, physical interpretation boards can be particularly obtrusive, spoiling the very thing that is the essence of the place. Yet without interpretation they may have little meaning to the visitor. A proportion of visitors will have a desire for in-depth information on a specific topic. Gardeners in particular will demand information about plants - their names, habitats, propagation etc. - that is far too great to put onto labels. Collections can benefit from telling the story behind each artefact, but have little space to do this.

Consider using numbers that the person inputs to their device like a traditional audio guide, but to have information presented to them as more than a commentary. Consider using QR codes, NFC tags or Beacons to trigger focused interpretation with very low visual impact.

Virtual Reality and Augmented Reality

Virtual and Augmented reality can involve expensive equipment and high-risk leading-edge technology. However, it can be as simple as a panoramic image, stitched together from old photographs that you look at and drag-to-move with a finger on your phone and compare to the present-day view. In other words, you can incorporate a VR or AR experience to whatever level of sophistication that you can, given the tools that you have.

Virtual Reality

Virtual Reality (VR)is immersion in an artificially created world. It is more the realm of games and simulation than interpretation, but can provide a unique experience. Imagine fighting a Roman gladiator or a lion in an arena, with a baying crowd looking on. Armed with a headset and an electronic sword (operated by accelerometers) you can give someone a surprisingly real experience of the fear and adrenaline rush that must have been felt by participants. It is too easy to dismiss such things as silly games. Simulators are used extensively to train airline pilots and astronauts, and the level of reality can be so good that the brain and the emotions do become completely immersed in the virtual world.

Augmented Reality

Augmented Reality (AR) is where you can see the real world but with something extra to 'augment' the view. Imagine a Roman fort or villa where in real life all that remains is the groundplan on which you are standing. Imagine that you now hold up your phone and looking through it you see the fort or villa from the perspective of where you are standing, but seeing it as it was in its heyday, perhaps with people moving around. As you turn or walk forward the 3D model view keeps pace, so you can peek around corners or into windows and watch life two millennia ago.

Maybe you are at the top of a church tower and use your phone to see the surrounding deserted medieval village in the grip of the Black Death, with the houses where everyone died slowly fading from the map. Maybe from the top of a hill fort you survey a graphic reconstruction of the very different Iron-age landscape. All through the window of your smartphone.

Downloadables

The ability to take things away, whether as information or as souvenirs is another powerful tool in the box. Most devices can download images and PDFs and will store them until the user deletes them.

Outdoor Trails

Outdoor trails are often far better downloaded onto a smartphone than as a paper leaflet. The smartphone is already carried by the visitor, and is more immune to the effects of rain and wind. Graphic design costs are the same, but there is no printing or re-printing cost. The advantages are:

- Cheaper to produce
- Easy to update
- Not spoilt by rain and damp
- No dispensers so not open to vandalism

Event leaflets

Promote your programme of events with downloadable event leaflets. The user can save comprehensive details on their phone. A downloaded leaflet is always to hand until deleted, and is more likely to be seen and used when a past visitor is trying to remember what is on and when.

Badges and tokens

The collection of badges and tokens for visiting specific places or undertaking specific tasks has a long history in religion and tourism. Although out of fashion, it is perhaps due for a digital makeover and revival. There are a number of ways of facilitating the collection of tokens or other artifacts, from simple number codes to enter manually, to the proximity triggers that are described in their own chapter. Things could be acquired for their own sake, such as stunning pictures for screen backgrounds, or to win a prize for a set, or as an educational game where information and an artefact is only revealed on completion of a task. The key point here is that the visitor is given some unique digital artefact that they can keep permanently as their trophy and memento.

Interactives

The underlying principle of interactives is very obvious, and easy to implement in a digital environment, but the creative possibilities lie in the ability to challenge the visitor and to respond to their needs. Interactives can create personalised experiences and can potentially create digital artefacts such as images that can later be shared via social media.

Building interactives requires some knowledge of web or app development, but these technical skills are based on common programming languages and are in good supply. Here are some basic ideas that can be run on relatively simple code, often Open Source, that can be copied and adapted to suit:

Custom map to download

Visiting a war cemetery where a relative is buried can be a difficult experience in terms of locating the correct grave and recording its whereabouts. One can make a database of names interact with an image so that you can be presented with a map, or aerial photograph, with a pin showing the location you are seeking (and potentially a dot showing your current GPS location). The map with its pin can be generated as a PDF, so that it is downloadable. The same technique could be used for an arboretum or a wildlife site where classes of flora and fauna are contained in a database that creates multiple location pins on a map. The key is that the individual database items have a data field for latitude and longitude and this is georeferenced to the map image.

Scratch-off images

Many venues have old photographs or paintings which can be matched with modern photographs that can then be 'scratched off' with a finger to reveal the underlying image. This can work with before and after images of restoration, reconstructions, or any kind of layered or time-series history, particularly in archaeology where aerial photography, LIDAR, and geophysics could be superimposed and scratched away (or added) in turn.

Green screen selfie

The trend for taking 'selfies' could be enhanced by providing a green screen background that can then be replaced on-screen by the visitor with an appropriate image from the venue. Possibilities include landscapes and settings, famous paintings, and being photographed with (or 'photo-bombed' by) people from the past.

Matching games

An educational game to match images with their correct name by dragging the images into the correct boxes. Subjects could be people, trees, architecture, animals, and it could be matching pictures - such as leaf and bark close-ups to a full-image of the right tree or matching pictures with names or descriptions. The boxes can be made to respond to show if they are correct or not, and the game could have a timer. You could offer small rewards to those who show a completed game with its 'success' screen and time.

Jig-Saw Puzzles

A simple and intuitive game to assemble an image by dragging jumbled-up pieces around the screen. The pieces can be made to snap to their correct positions to aid alignment, and when they are all in place some information is revealed, such as the story behind the image.

Geocache/treasure hunt

Geocaching has emerged and enjoyed much publicity in recent years. It is easy to give GPS co-ordinates to locations where a cache can be found, or just to provide clues in an old-fashioned treasure hunt. The smartphone provides a means to hunt via location technology. If you wish to make the game more formal and competitive, the smartphone has the means to capture and collect some form of electronic 'token', such as a photograph, or to scan a tag/beacon that registers and builds up a score. It could even show the trail of where the visitor has been.

Webcams

We have covered this subject in a dedicated chapter, but it is worth quickly reviewing some potential applications:

- Live webcam in a nest or burrow, with the ability to take away snapshots
- Daily auto-recorded highlights of last night's bat activity, or the dawn chorus
- Time-lapse of the construction of an iron-age roundhouse, or the restoration of a room
- Filming flowers and insects in the non-human-visible part of the spectrum that they use
- Showing live pond life through a microscope

Control of Narrative

Some venues have marvellous stories to tell. The existence of such a story means that the interpretation has the opportunity for suspense, surprise, and an unfolding narrative. Interpretation in such situations can benefit from being more like theatre or a play, than a museum visit.

It is much easier to control the unfolding of a narrative on a digital platform, where navigation can be controlled on the basis of 'you can't see this until you've seen that', or by the user taking some specific action, such as locating a hidden code, or by use of location or proximity technologies.

By contrast, the standard 'introductory' or 'overview' leaflet cannot prevent the visitor from skipping ahead and spoiling a thrilling 'denoument'.

Key Knowledge — A New Creative Toolbox

Digital media opens up an extended toolbox with which to be creative. Mobile digital enables you to take your interpretation into almost any environment.

Although technology may have a novelty value, this is short-lived. Content is king. You don't need to be cutting edge to have a 'wow!' factor, just desig good interpretation using the new toolbox.

Mobile digital can be discreet, immersive, interactive, and enables the 'augmentation' of reality.

New technologies tend to be over-hyped and don't live up to their inflated expectations, but do tend to be useful, once we discover how best to use them.

In a digital environment you can control the unfolding narrative more closely than with physical interpretation, thus achieving the dynamics of storytelling and drama.

Project Management

Success 12

Technology can be described as the application of scientific knowledge to everyday life. That application process does not always go smoothly and there have been many famous technological disasters. Still, most of us get excited and attracted by the promises of tomorrow's technology, as it feeds our hopes for a brighter future. At other times we may deeply resent the way that technology is forcing us to change, or making our lives more complex and risky. Our relationship with technology is thus a fairly complex one and may change over time, and be influenced by our world views.

Whatever our emotional reaction, technology is strategically important and is something that can and should be actively managed. That management brings with it the challenge of technical understanding; a challenge that may be particularly difficult for the artistic and creative mind that has not grown up among the many touchstones of science. Faced with this challenge, there is a natural tendency to delegate entirely to technical people. This is a mistake. Technical people will naturally tend to be technology enthusiasts, even 'geeks'. They may have a personal bias towards particular technologies. They may be suppliers with a commercial interest. More importantly they are unlikely to bring the broad outlook and strategic management skills that lead to sensible planning and decision-making. Managing technology does not require an in-depth technical knowledge. It does require some understanding of cause and effect, and the interplay between technology, people, economics and other factors that commonly make up the management gamut.

In terms of timing and where you should be, technology can be thought of as a moving wave. Jump in too early and you may suffer from instability and high cost, sometimes called the 'early adopter premium'. Join too late and your technology is quickly obsolete: you have missed the power of the wave. There is an optimum window, perhaps a little differently positioned for each organisation. Finding that 'sweet spot' is a part of technology management.

In order to avoid being drawn into general management techniques, which is well covered in many publications, we have focused specifically on why things go wrong in digital heritage projects. This is rather like the 'black box' approach of analysing accidents to identify and eliminate root causes.

Stage One - Planning and preparation

Expectation management

The public and the media love to dream about the future. In doing so, we can all too easily imagine a utopian future just around the corner, based on one tentative new idea. In reality, there is nearly always a lot of hard 'trial and error' development work, and an almost inevitable series of failures, between an idea and the advantages of the technology that we envisage from it.

While it is good to occasionally take modest risks on incremental developments, we should temper this with an understanding of the work involved and a realistic view of the risks of failure. Generally speaking it is best to limit your core functions to technology that is already working successfully in similar circumstances. At the same time you can look over the horizon and think and experiment in non-critical areas.

The system components approach

At some point, any technology will suffer a component part that either fails or becomes obsolete. This becomes a problem when the replacement component follows a later standard and is incompatible with what you already have. Most of us have seen this effect in our own computer equipment: an app update requires an OS update, which in turn requires hardware update, locking us into spending more than we intended. In the worst case, this cascade effect can mean that a minor failure of one component, which may be hardware or software, requires replacing everything in order to get back to a working system.

Ideally, system components should each do a discrete task and follow established standards for interoperability such that there is a choice of components, any of which can be made to work together. That way, if a component fails or is superseded, then it can be replaced with a different component with the same function and the system still works.

Proprietary versus open products

Vendors always like locking their customers into their products. One sale can then lead to a lifetime of income with the vendor setting the price. This is obviously to be avoided if you are a customer. Lock-in may prevent you shopping around, or from updating, and the long-term costs may escalate outside your control. Here are some examples of ways in which lock-in can be engineered:

- Rental rather than purchase
- Essential intellectual property that is licenced
- Proprietary systems or components that do not interoperate with similar ones
- Hardware and software that are locked together as one product
- Mandatory updates

It is important to seek out products and purchasing terms where cost and ownership are permanently under your control.

Testing

Most people trust technology far too much. Simple testing can identify things that are not going to work for you, and can reveal where assumptions have been wrong. You do not need to develop a complete installation, just something that is enough to prove the principles. If robustness over time is a concern, then trials and pilots should be undertaken before making a decision. Finding at an early stage those things that don't work is considerably cheaper than finding them at a late stage when commitments have been made. Testing should always be practical and under realistic conditions. An on-site 'walk through' simulation can reveal a surprising number of snags and improvements.

Knowledge seeking

In today's Internet age we are used to seeking instant knowledge online, but in contemplating a digital heritage project this should be extended from mere 'Googling' to actively interviewing and visiting others, gathering their experiences, and avoiding repeating their mistakes. Always try to see a technology in action and use it yourself. Speak with others who are already using the technology that you are considering. It is surprising how much valuable practical knowledge comes from the 'warts and all' experience of others.

Obsolescence

Technology is always changing. In some areas, and at certain times, it exhibits sudden spurts of change. If new models and new features have come out frequently in the past, then it is reasonable to assume that this will continue into the future. We use a 'vegetable' analogy for technology obsolescence. No matter how tasty they are on the day of purchase, but you would not expect vegetables bought months ago to still be edible.

Anticipating the likely rate of obsolescence of both capital equipment and software may be an important factor. This is particularly so if the equipment has to interface with other equipment or systems that may get updated and become incompatible. Stand-alone equipment has the advantage that it will continue to do its intended job, even though it may not have all the latest functionality.

Mission Creep

This is a well-known phenomenon, but it is still easy to fall into the trap. As we will see in the next section, flexibility and iteration is a positive technique. It is expanding the scope and ambitions of a project that causes shortfalls and unintended consequences. Be clear about what you are trying to achieve and make it into an agreed statement that becomes a permanent reference.

Iterative and 'agile' development

While it may seem convenient and very logical to plan then implement the plan exactly, new ideas, and unexpected issues often only come to light during implementation. In addition, during a long project, the requirements can actually change over time. An implementation phase should therefore be an iterative process as you learn and revise during implementation. This iterative process is well understood by engineers who build complex systems such as software. A concept called 'Agile Development' is based on launching a product as soon as it is functioning, no matter how crudely, so that it can be tried it out 'for real' and feedback used to improve the next iteration. This is preferable to designing and building to a fully-finished state, then launching only to find the snags and issues that could have been discovered earlier, when they would have been easier to overcome. Digital interpretation project are a complex system of people, knowledge, places and devices and will develop much more smoothly with a systems approach. For example it may be worthwhile developing content and testing early in a project and learn practical lessons rather than wait until content is embedded in physical infrastructure and then realise it is too late to incorporate simple changes without adding to the cost.

Stage Two - Implementation

Clear contracting

The nature of any technology should be specified in terms of the requirements that it is to deliver. It is worth pouring over the words used, the promises made, the schedule, and any interdependencies or critical processes. It is very common in a large project for delays to build up, either overtly or covertly. Making 'minor improvements' and 'mission creep' during building, can introduce a series of small consequences that pressurise the suppliers that are the last in the chain. Project management must be active and continuous. Building in 'deliverables' and testing stages are all a good discipline. Setting only one 'ultimate' deadline and expecting contractors to manage to that is a recipe for a hurried project delivered late, with a high failure risk.

Internal Communication

Most heritage venues rely on staff, volunteers, and friends to deliver the overall visitor experience. The introduction of new technology should be flagged up early with them, and any concerns actively elicited and addressed openly and honestly. Giving a project a name by which it can be known, and producing temporary newsletters or articles in regular newsletters can all help to give a sense of understanding and ownership among those who can make it work or fail. These people are the front line. They have to interact face-to-face with the visitor, so their knowledge and attitude is critical for success.

Working with engineers and creatives

The arts and sciences were historically almost synonymous, and creativity among the great figures of the past normally came with a 'polymath' scientific understanding. The arts and sciences have grown into very separate and specialist disciplines, having different approaches, cultural values, and methods of working. Reconciling the two can be a challenge in the area of digital technology, where they tend to clash more than most fields.

What follows is a crude generalisation, and arguably unjust stereotyping, but looking at extreme stereotypes perhaps serves to make the point that there are pitfalls waiting for you if you fail to get balanced input from both mindsets.

The 'Engineer'

The technical professional is too often left to design and produce alone, as no-one else feels technically knowledgeable enough to manage them or to challenge their proposals. The technical mind is not so good at understanding and designing for the emotive, and at times irrational, aspects of human behaviour. It is motivated by what is technologically 'cool'. Technical people tend to give overly-detailed information, and use jargon without realising that they have not conveyed much real understanding, and have not made it clear what is important. As they tend not to be 'people persons' they may also skip user testing and feedback. The result can be 'technology for technology's sake' or 'the medium becomes the message'.

The 'Creative'

The creative practitioners who skillfully pluck our emotional strings with engaging narratives, and make us truly think about and understand a subject, can be inspiring leaders, but often lack the practical skills and attention to detail needed in complex project management. They can have a severe blind spot when it comes to appreciating what will work or not in practice, and the need to keep within physical or budgetary constraints. Having sold everyone on their ephemeral 'vision', creative types may see hard technical limitations and process deadlines, as 'flexible' - a challenge even. As they keep thinking and innovating, they will want to change things, even when it is really too late. Their management style can be emotional and tension-generating. This can produce creative breakthroughs, but on complex projects it more often leads to a practical disaster.

Achieving balance and coordination

The arts and sciences both make vital contributions to success in interpretation. Unfortunately it is not easy to meld them into one because of the way that the two types of discipline work. They speak different professional 'languages'. As a result they, quite innocently, can misunderstand each other at critical points. This can happen even with the best of intentions on each side. Add some professional rivalry, pride, or arrogance, especially between separate, maybe competitor organisations working for a single client and the stage is set for clashes.

Setting aside any deliberate sabotage or politics, clashes are often the result of a lack of sufficient communication, or lack of common understanding of the information communicated. Respect and appreciation for the value of the 'other side' must underpin all communication.

One integration technique is to adopt a 'Unified Brief and Specification' approach, in which the objectives are stated in clear and simple language in a shared document. This should be a single 'living' document that is updated as the project progresses, deliberately leaving some 'wiggle room' as better ideas will come along. It should include any agreed parameters including dates, or at least the necessary order of sequential events as phases.

The document needs to be short so that it can be regularly reviewed line by line. At the same time it should include all the key parameters, as an appendix if necessary, so that there is no room left for misunderstanding or misinterpretation.

Another approach is to employ a single lead contractor, or a third-party project manager, or just appoint from your own people a dedicated manager who will continuously and very closely manage the process and provide a single conduit between the client (or clients) and contractors for all information. There are many project management tools, and formal tools can be a positive aid, but sometimes the structure and assumptions behind the tools drives the process, often in an over-complicated or time-consuming way, and they eventually become ignored as they are too cumbersome. The simplest tool that will do the job is often the best - sometimes it's just a list.

Training

All of us increasingly expect devices and software to be intuitive in use. However, there is a major difference between being an end user, who can reasonably expect to learn as they go, and being a system administrator. If you are about to take a commercial flight, you would not expect to need training to be a passenger, although they do tell you what to do in an emergency. However, you would expect your pilot and crew to know every system aboard the aircraft, including its failure modes, and to be well-drilled in how to cope with any emergency.

Few people ever want to invest time in training, and for some it may even invoke fears that relate to their school years. It is often better to talk about 'familiarisation', 'know-how' and 'how-to' rather than use the rather formal word 'training', but ultimately those piloting the technology should fully understand how to use it. Untrained administrators tend to spiral into an increasing muddle, make unclear calls to help desks, and often seek solutions to the symptoms because they cannot identify the underlying problem.

You should try to positively design training so that it is easy and informal. The use of posters in the staffroom or toilets, 'how to' videos shared online, experience-sharing discussions over lunch breaks, a quiz with a prize, can all contribute to knowledge building.

Stage Three - Post-implementation

Evaluation, learning and knowledge management

Every technological project is an opportunity to learn internally and to share externally with others, just as you have hopefully benefitted from the knowledge of others in Stage One. Activities such as writing an overview case study and hosting a demonstration and workshop will also help you to analyse and articulate what you have learned.

As staff change over time, unrecorded know-how will simply 'walk out of the door'. Get those involved with a development to write (and test) instruction documents, to write up articles, and to share their thoughts in workshops and discussion that are in some way recorded. As this means the individual investing time to help someone else who they may never meet, make sure that you set aside time and rewards for doing this. It can be a good area for interns and trainees to become involved as it is in itself a learning exercise, and they are less likely to be distracted by the demands of other responsibilities.

While qualitative and quantitative methods of evaluation are well described elsewhere, such as the interpretation planning handbook 'A Sense of Place', measurement is a key part of digital evaluation. Digital technology offers automated statistics to offer, from app downloads to web pages visited and games or challenges completed. Care is needed to be sure of exactly what it is you are counting. For example, web pages that have many elements may register a 'hit' against each element in your analytics, resulting in multiple hits for a single page access. This needs careful filtering to ensure that you are only counting real activity.

You need to design your evaluation plan during the planning stages in order to establish what you will want to measure and why. You may then able to establish baselines for 'before and after' comparisons. Don't forget that number of visits, recommendations, repeat visits, satisfaction surveys, and dwell time, can also be surrogate indicators of successful digital interpretation.

Disaster recovery

For obvious reasons, the unexpected is perhaps the hardest factor to manage. Almost anything could have an impact on a project: equipment obsolescence, loss of staff, failure of a supplier, budget cuts, or more serious incidents such as accident, fire, flood, theft, cyber or terrorist attack. The list is so long that you cannot hope to consider every eventuality, so you must make generic plans that help you to manage the likely effects.

Plan who will do what in any emergency and who will press the 'go' button to declare an emergency. Who will take charge, who will speak to the contractors, to the press, and who will manage internal communications and how. Make sure that everyone knows the plan and their role, and has rehearsed any processes they need to carry out. In the immediate aftermath of a problem everyone can become overloaded. It is worth investing a little time to anticipate normally easy things that can consume precious time when under pressure and stress, and possibly without normal facilities, and prepare them in anticipation. Contact lists, generic information about the organisation and the project, contingency and backup information, anything that is relatively easy to achieve under normal circumstances but may be difficult if all systems are down.

For the longer term, reserving some small contingency budget, or ring-fencing emergency funding or loans from another budget on an 'only if needed' basis is a good idea to prevent you becoming moribund if the situation requires emergency funding. The normal approvals processes are not designed for emergencies. Organisations have often found themselves with insufficient money to replace or repair equipment that consequently becomes inoperative.

Following standards, modularising system components, keeping meticulous files and backups (off-site and checked for validity) will help enormously in the event of a major disaster. Ensure that all work done by external contractors is delivered as original files. In other words, try to make sure that you are always in direct ownership and control of your project assets. Ultimately, the best defence against disaster is the ability to rebuild, from scratch if necessary.

Key Knowledge — Project Management

Ensure that expectations are realistic. Agree an overview planning document stating the objectives and outcomes. Divide them clearly into 'required', 'expected' and 'desired' so that there is no room left for assumptions. Stick to those goals.

Plan your project well, but do not force yourself to a rigid sequential plan. Try to 'plan to learn' and adapt as you go. Learn some 'agile' techniques.

Plan your system as separate components that could work together differently or could work independently. Use open standards, and avoid proprietary lock-in.

Share your goals and objectives rather than specifying too much too early. Your staff, volunteers, friends, and contactors may have great ideas that help you achieve your ends.

Seek advice from others who have done similar projects.

Balance creative and technical input and ensure that both types are working to the same plan.

Test early and regularly. Expect failures. Be prepared to propose changes if things do not work well, rather than trying to force them to work, or accepting marginal performance.

Manage closely and iteratively, and critically. Most failed projects only discover that they have gone astray at the very end.

Communicate clearly and constantly. Make sure that you plan for training of front of house staff and volunteers.

Make some time for evaluation and recording as you go along. It may prove invaluable knowledge for you and others. You may be asked to present your success story.

Plan how you will handle disasters. At least identify a route for recovery - and hope it proves a waste of time.

Jargon Buster

App

An application software. This can be:

- A 'native app' residing in the device
- A 'web app' that is accessed across the internet
- A 'hybrid app' that does a bit of both

The key factors that distinguish 'native' from 'web' are: a) where is the processing done: is it on the local device or the remote server, and b) where is the data stored: local or remote. The distinction is becoming increasingly blurred as an app might retain some logon credentials and auto-update its data, but also act as the interface to the online experience. Apps to do with banking and social media are mostly in this hybrid category as some work and storage is done locally, but online access is needed to interact. Your browser is also a kind of native app that does the task of helping you to interface with the web.

Beacons and BLE

Beacons is emerging as the generic term used for all Bluetooth Low-Energy (BLE) proximity triggers. Although these are based on Bluetooth technology, they are different to 'Bluetooth Enabled' data devices such as headsets. They function by blindly transmitting a signal, whether anyone is receiving it or not. This is analogous to a lighthouse signalling the presence of land to any and all marine travellers.

A sample Beacon

iBeacons are the Apple manufacturer's offering and transmit only an ID number. Eddystone Beacons are the Google product and can also be programmed to transmit some text, which can be a URL to direct a device to a web address. There are other possibilities for future configurations of beacons based on the full set of BLE standards.

Bring Your Own Device (BYOD)

The principle that most users now come equipped with their own sophisticated audio-visual hardware in their smartphones and tablets. This means that it no longer makes sense for a venue to buy and maintain generic audio-visual hardware. It also offers an alternative delivery medium.

Digital media

Early communication and recording media used 'analogue' principles - a variable attribute of a medium to represent real-world things such as sound waves or video. So, for example. magnetic tape varies the amount of magnetism along its length to represent the vibrations of the air caused by sound. The variations can be recorded and replayed to recreate the vibrations through a loudspeaker and hence reproduce the sound. The quality of analogue depends very heavily on the quality of the equipment. If in our magnetic tape example the motor driving the tape runs a just a bit too slow or to fast, the pitch of the playback will not match the original sound, and this will be very obvious. In addition, any external interference will add noise to the result.

Digital media translates the physical world (which is inherently analogue) into numbers that represent, for example, the sound waves or video images. This is known as analogue-to-digital or A/D conversion. These numbers are then easily stored, transmitted and even processed, using a variety of relatively cheap computing electronics. They can be accurately returned back to analogue. Faults and interference can to some extent be eliminated as each chunk of information has 'check digits' calculated from the data and appended to the chunk. For example, the total number of data bits that are 'zero' would constitute a simple check number. If the check digits transmitted with the data and the check calculated on the received data don't match, then the chunk of data can be re-sent until they do, or some other action can be programmed, such as skipping the distorted section. Digital systems tend to either produce accurate reproduction, or nothing.

Gartner hype cycle

The tendency for the advantages and impact of new technology to be over-hyped, leading to a phase of disappointment, but followed by a more realistic level of practical use. The concept was developed by the Gartner consulting organisation in the US.

See:
http://www.gartner.com/technology/research/methodologies/hype-cycle.jsp

GPS, GNSS, and Satnav

A method of locating the geographical position of a device by reference to signals from a constellation of satellites orbiting the Earth. The position can be obtained by an app or a web page in order to locate the device on a map. Several terms are used interchangeably. GNSS (Global Navigation by Satellite System) and Satnav are generic, while GPS (Global Positioning System) is the original US military system that popularised its use, so the name has stuck, despite there now being other systems in use.

HTML and HTML5

HTML (Hyper-Text Mark-up Language) has always been the main language in which most web pages are written. It contains the content, and the 'tags' that describe the types of content. HTML version 5 (HTML5) is the latest international standard that has been agreed by the W3C (World Wide Web Consortium). Of particular importance in HTML5 are rules about how web pages can interact with web apps and physical features in devices, such as Sat-Nav.

IP Address

The Internet and Web work by sending information in chunks known as 'packets' that are individually addressed to the receiving device. These packets then find their way through the complex networks that make up the Internet - a bit like a letter in the postal service. The addresses are known as Internet Protocol (IP) addresses. Traditionally they have four blocks of number digits, separated by a dot, with each block being up to three digits. They look something like this: 192.16.0.123.

With the growth of the Internet, the world is running out of these numbers and needs more functionality to cope with the number of devices and the range of uses. We are now moving to a longer address system known as IPv6, which has eight groups, separated by colons, with each block having up to four hexadecimal digits. They look something like this: 1080::8:800:200C:417A. Given the current size of the Internet, the old system, now referred to as IPv4, is likely to hang around for a long time, and we will have to provide for both systems, which may mean some incompatibilities. See also URL.

JavaScript and jQuery

JavaScript is a programming language that can be run inside a web page and is currently the best basis for constructing web apps, in conjunction with HTML5. When you look at a web page you often run short JavaScript programs that are embedded on the page. Going one step further, jQuery is a set of JavaScript programs bundled up as a library. This makes it easier and quicker for developers to build stable and reliable web apps by using components from the library.

Kiosk

A fixed hardware device that is secured to a wall or plinth for use by the general public. In the early years the technology of touch-screen kiosks was subject to a high level of failure, although the development of consumer touch-screen devices has led to vast improvements in robustness.

Newer kiosk devices use mobile-derived touch-screen principles such as 'drag' to move and 'pinch-to-zoom'. Older devices that navigate by 'scroll buttons' and off-screen track-pads etc. have been observed to confuse users. This shows how quickly users can change their skill-set due to the influence of frequently-used technology.

A sample Kiosk

Media and Rich Media

Media is the broad term for anything that is not text - such as images. Rich media means dynamic media such as audio, video, and interactives. Media files, especially rich media files, can be very large and this can cause problems with storage and transmission, unless care is taken to optimise them for the system they are used on. Competing formats and unstable or emerging standards further complicate the use of rich media.

NFC Tags

Near-Field Communication (NFC) is short distance radio technology that works like contactless payment cards. The user simply holds their NFC-enabled phone next to the tag and it will open their browser at the URL that is encoded into the tag. It is a 'passive' device, powered by a signal from the phone, so does not

A sample NFC Tag

need a battery and can work outdoors. You program tags via a programming app on your phone. During programming you have the option to electronically lock the tag so that it cannot be changed. NFC is not device or software specific, although the visitor must have a phone that lets them access NFC, and to have NFC switched on.

Operating System (OS)

Each computer hardware device needs a fundamental software, known as the Operating System, that acts as a kind of 'translator' between the 'high-level' applications that we interface with as users, and the 'low-level' machine instructions necessary to make the specific hardware do the tasks that the app requests. The OS is thus specific to the structure of the hardware. In turn, apps have to be written to work on a specific Operating System. For smartphones today the common Operating Systems are: iOS (Apple devices), Android (the Google system), or Windows (Microsoft). The future may see other systems emerge.

Phone networks and roaming

In your home country, your mobile phone will normally only connect to the network of your phone service provider. Geographical coverage is one of the factors on which networks compete, and that means that you only get a service when you are within range of one of your provider's masts.

Your monthly payment plan may also cover some or all of your home-network usage. If the data plan is limited, then using your phone in an unusual way, such as accessing many video tours, can push you over the limit and incur premium charges.

When travelling abroad, the networks have mutual arrangements to carry each other's traffic. Usage may have to be enabled in advance, but when it is, your phone may well be able to connect to several different networks that have a sharing agreement with your service provider. Ironically, this multi-network sharing can give you better coverage abroad than at home. However, both the remote network and your service provider look to make money for carrying calls or data. 'Roaming' charges are often excessive compared to the normal 'home' charges, and there are many horror stories of people incurring massive and unexpected bills. The things that may be included in your monthly payment plan are often chargeable at a high premium when roaming.

The complexity and alleged profiteering has caused concern among consumer groups and governments. The European Union (EU) has legislated against roaming charges within EU countries, so the situation when travelling within Europe has improved. However, the situation internationally is complex and this leads to consumer worries about phone usage abroad.

Sometimes it is best to buy a local 'Pay-As-You-Go' SIM card for the country you are travelling in. However, these tend to come with fixed limits so may not do everything you wish.

QR Codes

'Quick Response' or QR codes are two-dimensional barcodes and look like a chequerboard pattern. The user needs a QR code reader app on their phone. They initiate the app and point their phone's camera at the QR code, which is then 'read' by the reader app. If the deciphered QR code is a URL the app launches a browser and takes the user to the web page. There are many free online apps to generate QR code images from URLs, and you can print them on a normal printer, so they can have virtually no cost. They are compatible with all normal smartphones.

Screen reader

A software for the sight-impaired that reads 'out loud' the content on a web page. Screen readers work directly from the HTML code that creates the page. It is important when using images and other visual artifacts to provide a text alternative - sometimes known as an 'Alt' tag - which is not visible on screen, but which a screen reader will pick up from the code.

Uniform Resource Locator (URL)

This is a user-friendly name by which the location of anything on the Web can be found. The first part usually begins http://www to indicate that it is a web protocol URL. The main part of a URL, which might look like 'anyone.com' is known as the domain name, and is translated by the Internet's Domain Name Servers (DNS) into the IP addresses of the specific server on which that resource resides. There can be more than one URL pointing to a server. The rest of the URL (after the slash /) identifies the location of the resource within that server. A 'resource' can be many types of things, but are commonly either a web page or a file for downloading or playing. See also IP address.

Printed in Great Britain
by Amazon